Architect's Pocket Book of
KITCHEN DESIGN

In loving memory
of my husbands

Francis Baden-Powell
and
Michael Brawne

both architects and both cooks
and
for whom I designed kitchens

Architect's Pocket Book of
KITCHEN DESIGN

Charlotte Baden-Powell

WITHDRAWN
UTSA LIBRARIES

AMSTERDAM • BOSTON • HEIDELBERG • LONDON • NEW YORK • OXFORD
PARIS • SAN DIEGO • SAN FRANCISCO • SINGAPORE • SYDNEY • TOKYO
Architectural Press is an imprint of Elsevier

Architectural Press
An imprint of Elsevier
Linacre House, Jordan Hill, Oxford OX2 8DP
30 Corporate Drive, Burlington, MA 01803

First published 2005

Every care has been taken in the preparation of this book but neither the
author nor the publishers can be held responsible for any errors or
omissions, or for any results arising from such errors or omissions by any
person or body using this book

British Library Cataloguing in Publication Data
A catalogue record for this book is available from the British Library

Library of Congress Cataloguing in Publication Data
A catalogue record for this book is available from the Library of Congress

ISBN 0 7506 6132 1

For information on all Architectural Press publications
visit our website at www.architecturalpress.com

Working together to grow
libraries in developing countries

www.elsevier.com | www.bookaid.org | www.sabre.org

ELSEVIER   BOOK AID
            International   Sabre Foundation

Printed and bound in Great Britain

Contents

Preface

When writing the *Architect's Pocket Book* (first published in 1997), I realised that some subjects really could not be very well dealt with in only one or two pages. This was particularly so with kitchens, the design of which is a complex subject and which requires considerable detailed information.

So here is a pocket book about kitchen design which I hope will fill in the gaps. It is not a glossy manual, but rather a book of facts and figures which the designer needs to know. Architects know how to make things look stunning, but kitchens must also function well to be loved by their clients.

With the advent of television programmes and numberless books about gourmet cooking, more needs to be known about the room in which this is done.

Designers, be they architect, builder or homeowner do not necessarily have much cooking experience, so hopefully the planning procedures described will be of some help.

This book deals only with the design of *domestic* kitchens. Commercial kitchens are a specialist subject, catering for substantial numbers with a large workforce, so they bear little resemblance to a kitchen in the home.

The opening chapter is a brief summary of the long slow journey from open fireplace to modern cooker. It also shows the great social changes which have taken place in the last century which now enables one person, alone, to prepare, cook and clear away a family meal compared with the numerous servants needed in Victorian times.

The labour saving aspect of the modern kitchen has been made possible not only by the technological innovations of appliances and gadgets, but also by supermarket provision of prepared meals and pre-washed vegetables.

In the last few decades, little real innovation has been made in appliances since the introduction of microwave cooking. However, the design and performance have considerably improved, some having many sophisticated features. Many now give greater attention to green issues such as fuel consumption and use of eco-friendly materials.

Greater standardisation of cabinets and appliances, at least in Europe, has lead to a wider choice and the ability to 'mix and match' items from different manufacturers.

The kitchen today is truly the hub of the family home. It is a place where chores other than cooking take place, where children play or do homework, and where parents spend a great deal of time. It also is the room upon which most money is spent and so deserves special attention.

I hope you will find this book both interesting and useful and that the resulting designs will be admired both for their efficiency as well as their looks.

Charlotte Baden-Powell

Acknowledgements

I am greatly indebted to the many manufacturing representatives of kitchen fittings for their advice and help.

The magazine *Which?* was also a very useful source for objective advice about kitchen appliances.

The Bibliography lists my main sources, amongst which I would single out the small paperback *Kitchens* by John Prizeman as being a classic.

The DoE series *Spaces in the Home* and the *Architects' Journal Activities and Spaces* are also invaluable.

My thanks also to Mary Tapping and Margaret Rixson for help with typing the manuscript.

1
History of the kitchen

Designing kitchens necessitates the integration of functional requirements, together with spaces which are pleasant to work in. Before analysing these needs it is worth looking back in time to see the antecedents of the modern kitchen. This will help to articulate and clarify the different activities needed to prepare complex meals and to realise how radically modern technology has reduced both the space and manpower needed to achieve this.

Early kitchens

The earliest kitchens, all over the world, are simply open fires, most often out of doors which is still so today in countries with a climate hot enough all the year round to make this possible.

Central hearth with reredos in a croft Birsay in Orkney

In Britain, little is known about kitchens until Norman times. After the Romans left Britain in AD 407, the culinary arts were largely forgotten. Food was often cooked outdoors on cauldrons or spits. This was to avoid the risk of fire and to keep smells out of the houses.

The central hearth
In Saxon times, food was cooked on central hearths in large, high ceilinged halls. Smoke drifted out of unglazed windows or

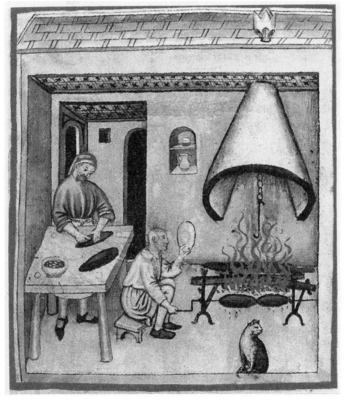

Turnspit rotating meat by hand – Italian manuscript (15th century)

a hole in the roof. Everyone ate communally on trestle tables, with the lord sitting at the centre of a table set across one end of the hall, overlooking his household who sat at tables placed along the hall before him. Later on, the lord's table was often raised on a dais to become, literally, a high table. Close by *cupboards*, i.e. boards for cups, displayed the gold and silver demonstrating his wealth. *Andirons* or firedogs were used to support the logs on the hearth and were later incorporated into the wall fireplaces, and became a useful way to support a roasting spit. These spits were at first operated by human *turnspits*. Later, various mechanical means were developed, including clockwork devices and treadwheels turned by dogs.

Dog acting as turnspit in an Inn in Newcastle Emlyn
Aquatint by Thomas Rowlandson 1797

The advent of the chimney

Soon after the Norman conquest, the fireplace moved to the wall although the central fireplace continued right up until the fourteenth century. Moving the fireplace to an outside wall may have come about because of the impossibility of having a central fireplace in a building of more than one storey. This allowed the development of the flue to carry away the smoke up to the outside air. At first these flues were funnels cut diag-onally through the thick walls to an opening higher up on the outside of the wall. Later, tall cylindrical shafts were developed. The word 'chimney' comes from the old French *cheminée* meaning the fireplace or hearth, not the flue as in current usage. Despite the enormous advantage the chimney brought to eliminating smoke from the room, a tremendous amount of heat and smells was generated from spit-roasting meat for several hundred people. So from the fourteenth century, kitchens began to be separated from the great halls. These medieval kitchens were large with high ceilings, some-times ventilated by louvers in the roof. A fine example of this can be seen in the Abbot's kitchen at Glastonbury.

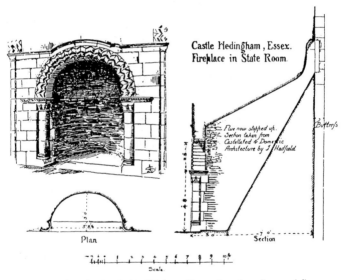

Norman fireplace in Castle Hedingham Essex showing diagonal flue c. 1140. Drawing by L.A. Shuffrey from *The English Fireplace*

Fuel

Timber, preferably hardwood, was burnt on the fires, while the poor used dried dung and peat. In the sixteenth century, wood

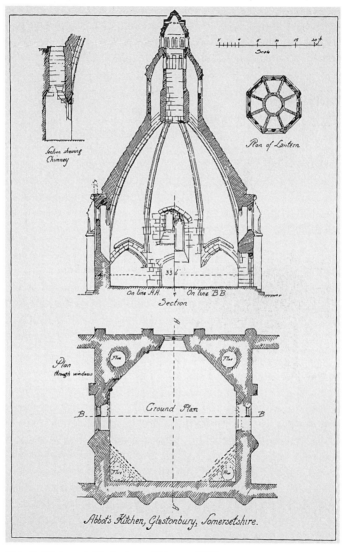

Abbot's kitchen at Glastonbury Abbey c. 1340.
The four corner flues were gathered into the octagonal lantern
Drawing by L.A. Shuffrey from *The English Fireplace*

became scarce and *seacole* came into general domestic use. It was called 'seacole' because it was brought to London and the east coast towns by boat from the open cast pits in Durham and Northumberland. Coal cannot be burnt directly on a hearth, so the basket grate was developed to hold the coals.

Early ovens

The first ovens were spaces made under brick or stone hearths, but they were soon moved into the return side walls of the open fireplace. These ovens, which can still be found in old cottages, were to bake bread. A fire was made inside using faggots and the door left ajar to allow the smoke to escape up the chimney over the adjacent fire. When the brick-lined oven was hot enough, the ashes were raked out and the loaves baked in the residual heat.

Development of the range

There were no innovations in ovens until the invention of the range, which was developed in the eighteenth century by men who were not professional stove makers but inventors such as Benjamin Franklin, Count Rumford and the missionary Philo Stewart.

In the late eighteenth century Count Rumford, an English physicist raised in America but living in Europe, wrote several far-seeing essays on the construction of kitchen fireplaces and utensils. He put forward the first idea for a kitchen range to supersede the open fire. He designed one fireplace for a Bavarian nobleman, which had several small fireplaces hollowed out of the masonry, and arranged in a horseshoe plan. The cook could stand in the middle and attend his pots, which were sunk into holes over the fires. By 1800, he had designed small cast iron ovens for poor families, and proposed roasting ovens set in masonry over a small fire below. He suggested the use of steam for cooking and also economising on heat by using stacked pans. Twin-walled steamers were suggested for the purpose of containing heat more efficiently.

Count Rumford's design for a kitchen for a Bavarian Nobleman 1797.
Built of massive brick providing insulation. Pans were fitted into
the top over an individual firebox with door to regulate air intake.
Two roasting ovens and a hot water boiler were also included

By 1840 the range had been developed as a separate piece of furniture which no longer needed to be built into masonry. Sometimes, in larger houses, the range was brought into the centre of the kitchen, leaving the open fire in the old wall fireplace for roasting.

The Victorian kitchen

The Victorians still thought it desirable to keep the kitchen, with its attendant smells, well away from the gentry end of the house. In grand homes, kitchens were positioned in the centre of the servants' wing, surrounded by the smaller rooms of the scullery, larder and pantry with separate stores for game, fish, ice and coal. These would be adjacent to the servants' hall with separate rooms for the cook, butler and housekeeper.

Great kitchen in the upper ward of Windsor Castle c. 1855.
The kitchen has been modernised by bricking up the fireplaces at the side leaving only one oven at the far end wall. Gas lighting has been installed over the work stations

The importance of the house could be judged by the number of chefs presiding over numerous kitchen maids. Kitchens were full of cooking devices such as roasting ranges, stewing and boiling stoves, turnspits and hot cupboards. However, there were no mechanised devices for washing, ventilation or refrigeration. Water was pumped by hand into scullery sinks and food was kept cool in an *ice box* with ice brought in from an *ice house* outside. Most food was still kept in north facing larders with natural ventilation.

The big change in kitchen design came about due to the social implications of the industrial revolution and the development of mechanisation.

Three iceboxes dating from 1800

Catherine Beecher

Alongside these early technological innovations, society was changing fast due to the advent of the industrial revolution which provided work for country girls who would otherwise have gone into service for middle class families. These social trends were recognised in America by a truly remarkable woman called Catherine Beecher (sister of Harriet Beecher Stowe). She was a reformer and early feminist. In 1841 she published a *Treatise on Domestic Economy*, which was a text book for girls schools which met with great success. She blamed many women's disappointments on the fact that they were not trained for their profession. She also remarked on the paradox of having servants in a democratic society, and suggested that housework should be divided up amongst members of the family. In 1869, she wrote *The American Woman's Home* in which, with amazing foresight, she proposed a kitchen where the central table and isolated dresser have disappeared. Instead she has a row of compact working surfaces arranged at waist height along the wall, properly lit by windows. To avoid discomfort in the hot American summers and because, unlike in Europe, bread was still mainly baked at home, the range was positioned in a separate room divided from the preparation area by sliding doors.

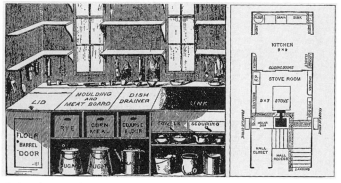

Kitchen layout advised by Catherine Beecher in 1869

Gas cooking

Gas cookers were invented in the first decade of the nine-teenth century but were not in general use until 1850. At first they were regarded with great suspicion – people feared explosions, poisoning or food tasting of gas. To begin with they were used in hotels and institutions, but it was not until 1924 that an oven regulator or thermostat appeared which made possible, for the first time, the accurate control of the temperature of the oven. The other great advantage was that the gas cooker did not need a flue, so could be placed any-where within a room, even in a room without a fireplace.

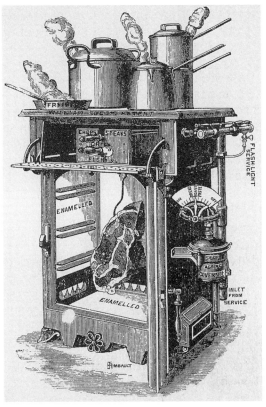

Charing Cross gas kitchener c. 1850

Electric cooking

Electric cooking appeared in England in 1890, but was slow to develop due to the sporadic nature of the electrical network. However, as electricity became more generally available at lower prices, electric cookers slowly began to be more commonplace, but were not in general use until 1930.

Electric kitchen at the Chicago Exhibition 1893

Appliances with electric motors

Before domestic electric appliances could be developed, two prerequisites were needed: a reduction to a compact, moveable size, and the introduction of a small built-in electric motor with a sealed motor housing and thermostatic controls. It was not until these were available that refrigerators, ventilator fans and washing machines were made possible.

In 1860, Ferdinand Carré produced a forerunner of the *refrigerator* using ammonia as its refrigerant, but it was not until the 1920s and 1930s were these in general production. Indeed, it was not until World War II that the *freezer* was developed.

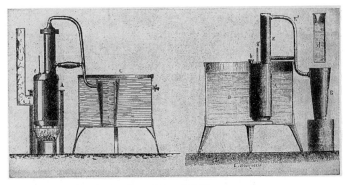

Refrigeration plant by Ferdinand Carré 1860

Similarly, a hand-turned *dishwasher* was patented as early as 1865 but it had to wait until the 1940s before modern dishwashers were mass produced.

Waste disposers or 'electric sinks' as they were curiously called at first, were invented in 1929 and in production in the US by 1935.

Early twentieth century

During the early part of the twentieth century up until the outbreak of World War I, kitchen design progressed very little. Then the supply of female servants dwindled dramatically as many found work in factories, which many women preferred as it brought in more money and gave them greater independence. So, gradually, the middle classes had to start managing without so much help. New gadgets and equipment were invented and the old cast iron ranges were replaced with gas or electric cookers. In the 1930s, the well-insulated solid fuel Aga and Esse cookers were developed, and were often adopted where mains gas was not available.

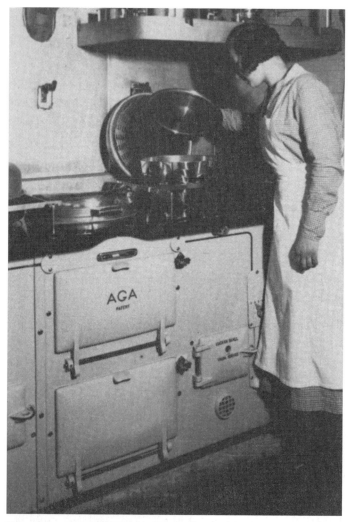

First AGA cooker – patented in Sweden by the inventor Gustav Dalén in 1922.
Photo: courtesy of the AGA archives, Sweden

The continuous worktop

The big change in the layout of kitchens came with the introduction of the continuous built-in worktop lining the kitchen
walls, as opposed to centrally placed, free-standing tables. One
forerunner of this phenomenon was the late nineteenth century pantry. Here we see the prototype with continuous waist-
high counters, a built-in sink with cupboards underneath and
cabinets with sliding doors hanging on the walls above.

Typical pantry 1891

In Europe, the new architecture of the 1920s re-appraised the house plan and based its findings upon functional rather than decorative criteria. In 1923, the Bauhaus exhibited a one-family house called 'Das Haus am Horn'. Here the L-shaped kitchen had a storage centre with the sink and sideboard placed along the wall. The sideboard was split into two elements – a base cabinet and wall cabinets. The worktop continued round the corner, flush up to the gas cooker, which had another worktop on the other side.

'Das Haus am Horn' in the Bauhaus Exhibition 1923

In 1927, J.J.P Oud designed low-cost kitchens for houses in the Weissenhof Siedlung in Stuttgart. These kitchens had a large window and an L-shaped run of continuous worktops with a preparation area, a sink, a food chest vented to the outside and a refuse can emptied from the yard. The cooker was placed to the left of a hatchway communicating directly with the dining room.

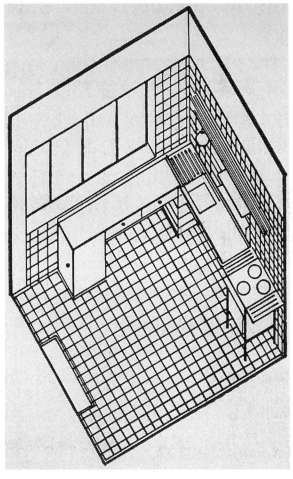

Kitchen by JJP Oud for the Weissenhof Siedlung, Stuttgart 1927

1920s and 1930s

In the late 1920s and early 1930s, furniture manufacturers found a ready market for kitchen cabinets. These were designed to hold almost everything the cook needed, complete with flour bins, egg racks and extending tables. They also often had vented compartments as refrigerators were still uncommon. From 1932–34 in the USA, General Electric and Westinghouse opened cooking institutions. Engineers, chemists, architects, nutritionists and professional cooks studied all aspects of the kitchen. The work process was scientifically investigated, and the way was opened for the modern streamlined kitchen.

A so-called 'Planned' kitchen by Hygena in the 1930s which cost £35. The units were finished in cellulose enamel 'in any colour or combination of colours'

The only heat storage cookers

★
AGA Model C is suitable for most households. Larger models for schools, restaurants, etc.

★
ESSE Fairy, the model for the small family's requirements. Larger models also available.

AGA and ESSE—the famous cookers with exceptional advantages. Economy—fuel consumption never rises. Perfect cooking and absolute cleanliness. At cooking heat night and day, they cope with the most irregular meal-times without increasing fuel bills. They need attention only once every twelve hours. They are backed by first-class Service Departments for repairs and adjustments. How lucky are the people who own an Esse or an Aga these days ! There are some still available, despite present manufacturing restrictions. If you would like one, enquire at one of the addresses below.

the only heat storage cookers

HEAT ACCUMULATING, THERMOSTATICALLY CONTROLLED, CONTINUOUS BURNING, INSULATED COOKERS

AGA Registered trade mark of Aga Heat Limited (Proprietors : Allied Iron-founders Ltd.). Showrooms : 20 North Audley Street, London, W.1.

ESSE Registered trade mark of Smith & Wellstood Ltd. (Proprietors of the Esse Cooker Company). Showrooms : 63 Conduit Street, London, W.1.

In 1940, a mutual desire to support the war effort made AGA Heat Ltd in London and its rival, the ESSE Cooker Co. in Scotland combine forces to promote their cookers. Courtesy of the AGA Food Service Group archives

1940s

In the early 1940s, three work centres were defined: storage and preservation; cleaning and preparation; cooking and serving. These studies were continued at Cornell University in the 1950s, where the concept of the kitchen *triangle* emerged. That is the relationship of the three most used appliances, i.e. sink, cooker and refrigerator. Recommendations were also made for the heights of worktops, the bottom of sinks and optimum levels for shelves.

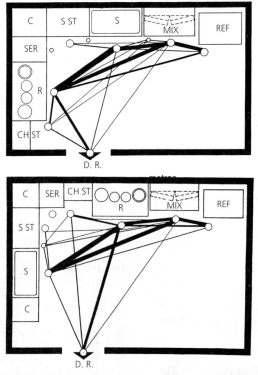

Travel lines shown in two different kitchen layouts. The travel cost in the lower plan is 29 yards longer than in the top plan according to *Guides for Arrangement of Urban Family Kitchens* by Heiner & Steidl of Cornell University published in 1950

Post World War II

After World War II, servants, for all but the grandest house-hold, had largely disappeared, having been called up for active service and finding more lucrative employment in industry when returning home. As has been shown, the introduction of efficient labour-saving devices and ergonomically designed kitchens had taken away a large part of the drudgery of kitchen chores. Now, however, the housewife, often left alone for much of the day, felt isolated from the rest of the house. Was it necessary for the kitchen to be so isolated? Efficient extractor fans dealt effectively with eliminating smells. With cabinets well made with hardwearing, easily cleaned surfaces, the kitchen began to be a room to be proud of and a status symbol in its own right. As early as 1934, Frank Lloyd Wright joined the kitchen, called by him 'the work space', to the living room. For the first time we are allowed discrete glimpses of the kitchen through a low-height partition of open shelves.

Glimpse of the kitchen from the dining area of the living room in the Malcolm Willey House, Minneapolis, Minnesota by Frank Lloyd Wright 1934

The demise of the isolated kitchen is also linked with the gradual abandonment of the formal dining room, which instead was more often replaced by a kitchen/dining room. The kitchen now has become the active centre of the household where the family can meet, eat, work and play. Parents can supervise young children and entertain visitors while keeping an eye on the cooking. So we arrive almost full circle back to Saxon times when everyone gathered round the central hearth. Cabinet makers and appliance manufacturers together have developed kitchens to suit the most modest needs right up to the most expensive fantasies. Today the kitchen is the most highly serviced room in the house, and the room on which most money is spent.

2
Types of kitchen

First considerations

How will the kitchen be used and by whom? What are the clients' particular requirements, if any? While considering these requirements, remember that the basic layout of the kitchen may last considerably longer than the present occupiers of the house and, therefore, should not be so idiosyncratic as to devalue the property. For instance, although it is common knowledge that kitchens are frequently ripped out and revamped, the general disposition of the entrance door, main window, position of sink and cooker if needing a flue, will largely condition future layouts unless substantial re-building is undertaken.

Questions to be asked
- How many people will the kitchen serve?
- Will all meals be served and eaten within, or adjoining the kitchen
- Or should there be a 'breakfast bar' in the kitchen with a more extensive dining area nearby?
- Is the person, who does most of the kitchen, tidy and able to work in a relatively compact area, or would they prefer a more generous layout?
- Do the clients have a once-a-month massive shop, and therefore require a large area of food storage, or even a separate larder?
- Or do they live conveniently near shops and buy food frequently, and can therefore manage with a relatively small area of food storage?

Cost

Determine whether quite basic cabinets and appliances are required, or whether no expense should be spared. If funds are limited, advise clients not to economise on the initial provision of plumbing and electrical installations so that some appliances may be added later when more money is available.

The family kitchen

The family kitchen is the key room in the house. It not only has to deal with cooking and eating, but may entail the supervision of children, whether toddlers playing on the floor, school-age children doing homework on the table or playing in the adjacent garden.

It should have links with the outside for access to dustbins and to any outhouses which may have a second fridge-freezer. Where there is a garden, a sheltered paved area could be provided for cooking and eating outdoors, and vegetable and herbs grown for the kitchen. Ideally, the kitchen should not be too far from an outside door to reduce the distance needed to carry shopping.

In the case of the dining-kitchen, the dining area should be accessed first so as to avoid guests walking through the not-necessarily pristine cooking area.

Many clients underestimate how much time is spent in the kitchen by all the members of the family, and wish to tuck the kitchen away in a dreary, north-facing room whilst giving pride of place to the formal dining room which, often, is only used a few times a year. Except for the super-rich who can afford staff or employ outside caterers, a separate dining room has largely become an anachronism for most families. The separate dining room also involves considerably more work in laying and clearing the table. In this respect, where kitchens are being installed in existing buildings, two adjacent rooms opened up into one makes the serving of meals and the supervision of children far simpler.

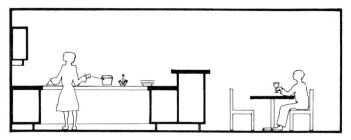

Kitchen screened by taller cabinets. Cabinets serving dining area set 300 mm higher than kitchen worktop conceal inevitable mess arising from dishing up

One essential device for the kitchen-dining room, which cannot be overestimated, is to have a barrier between the cooking and dining area which is a minimum of 1.2 m high. This can take the form of a back to counter unit with a shelf on top or storage cupboards of this height facing the dining area (see above). This device screens the kitchen counters when seated at table, and hides the inevitable mess created when serving up a meal.

The luxury kitchen

At the top of the market, the kitchen becomes a status symbol which can cost anything from £70–500,000 equipped perhaps with a range cooker, larger and more expensive than a Mercedes-Benz SLK car.

This type of kitchen may have vast refrigerators and ice machines from the USA, fan refrigerators which are better at circulating air, wine coolers, and even a separate cold room reminiscent of the north-facing larders of old country houses.

This phenomenon has largely been inspired by celebrity TV chefs who have renewed an interest in cooking from good raw materials. The rich, who like to cook, want a great room to do it in which will not only look good, but be a show place for the latest gadgets such as steam ovens, cappuccino machines, glass-covered plasma screen televisions and stainless steel-lined copper pans. These will be set in a decor of hardwearing, expensive finishes such as limestone floors and oak cabinets and granite or composite stone worktops.

There, more than ever, the kitchen is truly the heart of the home, and is where the party not only starts but continues.

Kitchens for flats

Kitchens in flats differ from kitchens in houses in that they may not be on the ground floor.
Waste disposal should be made easy, possibly with refuse chutes.
Care should be taken to provide good sound insulation, particularly if they are positioned next to bedrooms (including neighbours') as machines can vibrate and be noisy.
If the kitchen is to be installed in an old building with suspended timber floors, then provision must be taken to waterproof the floor against accidental leaks from appliances.

Inevitably, flat kitchens may have to accommodate laundry machines as space may be limited elsewhere but, if at all possible, try to locate these machines in or near the bathroom or bedrooms. Where a condensing dryer is installed in a kitchen, then an additional extractor fan over the dryer may be needed to deal with the resulting condensation.

Small, low-cost kitchens

Where space is at a premium, the choice of appliances must be considered first. A hob with a single oven built in underneath the counter will take up less room than a double oven built into a tall cabinet with a separate hob. Fridge/freezers come in many combinations so that the ratio of refrigerator to freezer can be to choice – possibly with a freezer situated elsewhere. For the really small kitchen, the narrow under-counter refrigerator with integral icebox is one choice and, for the bedsitting room there are mini iceboxes which can sit on the counter, large enough to contain a little milk, butter and cheese.

Busy people may not want an oven at all, and will be satisfied with a versatile combination microwave, perhaps augmented by an electric frying pan, jug kettle and toaster. The disadvantage of such a solution is that it may devalue the property for future owners.

Avoid sinks without drainers. Even the smallest draining area will help to contain water puddles on the worktop. Wall-hung wire plate racks, fixed above the sink or drainer, can increase the draining area without extending the worktop. Where there is space for a dishwasher, narrow models are available (see p. 135). For inexpensive cabinets, see p. 144.

Kitchen in a cupboard

For the rock bottom priced kitchen, an 'off the peg' counter-top, available from DIY superstores, with a sink unit and open shelves above and below, will save the cost of cabinets but will be subject to grease and dust and look untidy.

There are bespoke 'mini-kitchens' prefabricated with various combinations, which are not cheap but worth studying for ideas. It will generally be cheaper and more desirable, but not quicker, to design a more client-specific combination instead. These can be concealed with sliding or folding doors, which could also form part of a storage wall where the depth of the cupboard is suitable for clothes-hanging space alongside.

Stainless steel mini-kitchen by Space Savers 1000 w × 600 d × 2000 h.
Other combinations include microwave ovens.
Can be customised as required

Kitchens for the elderly

Older people who are not fully mobile and who may prefer to sit on a chair with castors while preparing and cooking meals, will need the worktops, appliances and socket outlets set at a lower level.

Cookers and refrigerators built into tall cabinets should also be positioned at a lower level and conversely dishwashers, washing machines and dryers should be set higher above the floor to access the interiors more easily.

Base and wall cupboards without doors make the contents more accessible and a knee-hole under the sink can make washing up and vegetable preparation easier.

Carousel shelves in corner cupboards and small free-standing carousel shelves on a worktop can also help.
Free-standing vegetable racks on castors can be stored under counters, and narrow wire basket shelves can be fitted to the inside of cabinet doors.

For more details of kitchens for the disabled and for wheel-chair users, see pp. 45–53.

3
Planning

Work sequence

The work sequence describes the order of activities from the unloading of food through storage, preparation, cooking and washing up, which can be described as follows:

1 Store   unloading and unwrapping of food, storing in refrigerator/freezer/larder/cupboards
2 Wash   washing, peeling, chopping, sieving food, dishwashing
3 Prepare weighing, mixing, cake and pastry making
4 Cook   hob for boiling and frying, grill for grilling and browning, oven for baking and roasting, microwave oven for defrosting, fast cooking and re-heating
5 Serve   dishing up food, keeping food hot, toasting bread, storing cutlery, crockery and condiments
6 Eat   table laying and eating

After this sequence is complete, there is the return sequence as follows:

Clear   removing dirty dishes to sink and dishwasher, returning uneaten food to refrigerator and cupboards
Wash up   waste disposal, loading dishwasher, hand washing, draining, putting away

One can see from the diagram that some cross-circulation is inevitable, as the sink is needed both for preparation and washing up. Likewise, storage of food will be in the refrigerator and in the dry goods cupboards.

The sequence preferred is normally planned from left to right or in a clockwise direction, but this is not essential and may be the prejudice of right-handed people. The left-hand cook may prefer a reverse order.

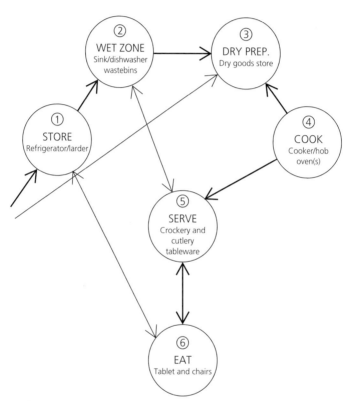

Work sequence

The heavier arrows indicate the main direction of activity. However quite a lot of cross circulation is inevitable – particularly when initially storing goods either in refrigerator or the dry store. Also the flow of crockery to and from the dishwasher and the table. The Wet Zone and the Dry Preparation area are interchangeable particularly as the worktop between the wet zone and cooking should be unbroken for ease of transfering heavy pans from sink to hob.

The work triangle

From the work sequences described above, it will be seen that there are three activities which relate to three main appliances – the refrigerator, the sink and the cooker. The relationship of these three fittings is commonly referred to as the *work triangle*.

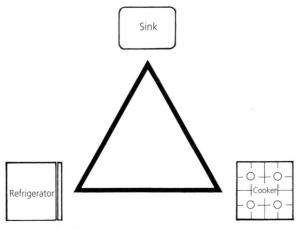

Kitchen triangle
Optimum length between 3.6 m and 6.6 m.
Less than 3.6 m means worktop length too short.
More than 6.6 m is time consuming and hard on the feet

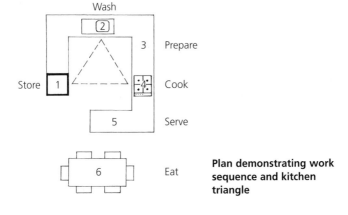

Plan demonstrating work sequence and kitchen triangle

The total length of the three sides of this triangle, measured from the centre front of each appliance, should not be less than 3.5 m or more than 6.5 m long. If the distance is shorter, then the work surface will be insufficient. If the distance is longer, then too much walking will be involved, making the whole process slow and exhausting.

Avoid circulation through the triangle – especially between the sink and cooker. These should be connected with a continuous worktop not longer than 1.8 m so as to limit the distance of carrying heavy pots, filled with liquid, between the two.

From this will be seen that the small, relatively compact, kitchen is easier to work in than the traditional large farmhouse kitchen. It is also evident that the 'U'-shaped plan satisfies these requirements best where the cook, centrally placed, can swivel round with very little movement between the three appliances, with continuous worktops uninterrupted by circulation routes or tall cupboards.

Where circulation does have to divide the kitchen, as in a two-sided or *galley* kitchen, then the sink and cooker should be kept to the same side.

The island kitchen, much loved by futuristic designers, often full of gleaming state-of-the-art gadgets, is the least satisfactory arrangement as it entails an excessive amount of walking, needs a large area of circulation space all round and has an insufficient amount of work surface and storage space.

Never interrupt the triangle with tall units.
Group tall units together at the end of a worktop run.

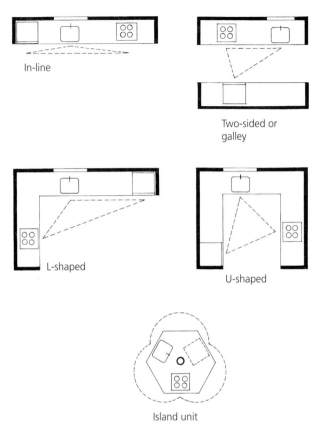

In-line

Two-sided or
galley

L-shaped

U-shaped

Island unit

Kitchen layout

These diagrams show different layouts with the kitchen *triangle* in a
dotted line.

This links the three most used appliances: sink, cooker and refrigerator.

The *U-shaped* kitchen is the easiest to use as the appliances surround the
cook and are set in worktops unbroken by circulation.

Conversely the *island unit* generates too much walking while having totally
inadequate amount of worktop space.

A good test for checking the efficiency of a kitchen is to exam-
ine the steps needed to make a pot of tea. This seemingly simple task is in fact a complex manoeuvre which involves most
parts of the kitchen as follows:

Making a pot of tea

- First, fill a kettle of water from the sink and turn it on, if electric, or take to the hob
- Fill teapot from tea caddy and fetch sugar bowl from dry goods cupboard
- Take cups, saucers and teapot out of cupboard, and teaspoons from cutlery drawer, and place on tray
- Fetch milk jug from refrigerator
- Pour boiling water into teapot, place on tray and carry to table.

Note that warming the teapot first, once a mandatory part of the ritual, is now no longer considered necessary in the properly heated kitchen.

Ergonomics

The dictionary definition of *ergonomics* is defined as 'the study of man in relation to the environment and the adaptation of machines and general conditions to fit individuals, so that they may work to maximum efficiency'. Nowhere is this more applicable than in the kitchen.

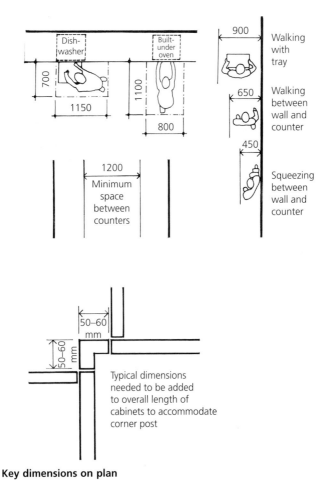

Key dimensions on plan

Key dimensions on plan

Allow a minimum of 1200 mm between parallel countertops. This is needed for two people to pass one another and for access when kneeling down to base cupboards and under-counter appliances.

See the diagram for the minimum dimensions for space in front of low level ovens and dishwashers.

The minimum clear doorway dimension for carrying a tray so as not to graze knuckles is 850 mm, ideally 900 mm.

Minimum space for walking between a counter and a vertical surface is 650 mm. Squeezing between the two is 450 mm.

Key vertical dimensions

The height of cupboards, drawers and shelves should be set at levels to minimise bending down or stretching up too far. Heights between +750 mm and +1550 mm are comfortable to reach.

The maximum upward reach (for a woman) when standing in front of a counter to access shelves is +1950 mm increasing to +2000 where there is no worktop.

Average eye level for men and women is 1567 mm.

Worktop heights

There has been much controversy about the ideal height for the kitchen countertop – not least because it has to suit women (average height +1650 mm) and men (average height +1740 mm).

Recent studies suggest that the standard height of +900 mm is too low, and could be increased to +950 mm or even +975 mm. While it is true to say that it is more comfortable to work at a worktop that is too high rather than too low, worktops also have to suit elderly people whose height has shrunk, and not yet fully grown children. So in this respect the +900 mm height is not a bad compromise.

However, should tall clients want the worktops raised, this is simply done by increasing the plinth (toe recess) height. Conversely, lowering the height below +900 mm is now not really feasible as under-counter appliances have a more or less standard height at +850 mm. So, more important than the precise worktop height is the *underside* of the worktop which should not be less than +870 mm. The finished worktop height is then determined by the thickness of the worktop itself which, depending upon construction, is likely to be between 30 and 50 mm.

Worktops should project at least 20 mm in front of the base cupboard doors so as to allow hand or bin space to collect crumbs and to prevent drawer handles from pressing uncomfortably into the cook.

There is a school of thought that suggests the sink top should be some 50 mm higher than the surrounding worktops so as to raise the bottom of the sink bowl to a more comfortable height. But the resulting change in worktop levels can cause breakages, and does not allow heavy pans to be slid from sink to hob. Similarly, such tasks as hand whisking in a bowl are easier to do at table top height of +740 mm. But the advent of electric dishwashers, whisks and food processors has reduced considerably the amount of time needed to do these jobs, so the argument for higher sinks is less valid.

Having said that, there are still some occasional lengthy chores such as shelling peas or cutting up oranges for marmalade, which are more comfortable to do sitting down. So, in addition to the larger table, a small table outside the area of the kitchen 'triangle' would be an asset. An easier alternative is to use the adjacent dining table, covered with a protective cloth.

Cabinets: dimensions to note

A continuous toe recess at the bottom of all cabinets should be provided. This should not be less than +100 mm high and 75 mm deep.

Knee recesses under worktops should be at least 460 mm wide by 500 mm deep, and not lower than 150 mm below a worktop.

Wall cupboards should not be fixed lower than 400 mm above a counter, otherwise they will obscure the back of the counter.

Wall cupboard doors should not be too wide – 400 mm is the ideal maximum width to reduce the chance of banging one's head on a door if left open. Similarly in a narrow, two-sided kitchen, base cupboard doors should not be too wide.

Appliances: planning considerations

Waist-high mounted appliances, such as ovens and refrigerators, save backache and give a better view into the machines.

As these will be fitted into tall cabinets, they will reduce the amount of worktop surface, so may not be suitable for the smaller kitchen.

Free-standing under-counter appliances can be mounted on castored platforms. Note that this may mean a higher worktop height. This is to make them easier to pull out for servicing, particularly useful for laundry machines, which often require frequent attention.

Although 'fully integrated' under-counter appliances such as ovens, refrigerators and dishwashers, are always more expensive than free-standing equivalents, the aesthetic advantage of having matching door fronts on an unbroken plinth line cannot be over-emphasised. How many otherwise attractive kitchens has one seen ruined by the one white-fronted appliance looking like a bad tooth with dirt-catching gaps alongside, spoiling the whole effect.

Energy labels

In 1994, the EU introduced *energy labels* which by law must be displayed on all electric ovens, dishwashers and cooling appliances (also washing machines, tumble driers, air conditioners and lamps). The virtue of this system is that it persuades the consumer to buy the most energy efficient appliances that will save running costs while at the same time protecting the environment.

In addition to this label, there is also the *Energy Star* which is primarily designed for office equipment. This shows that the product is capable of monitoring as to how often it is used, and, if not much activity is taking place, going into sleep mode thus keeping energy costs down.

There is also the *Energy Efficiency Recommended* label run by the Energy Saving Trust (EST) which is a quick way to identify energy efficient appliances. This logo indicates not only that the product is 'A' rated on the EU energy label but also that the EST conducts spot checks to ensure the classification is correct.

The *Eco-flower*, not yet very often found, may also be displayed. This means the product has been independently assessed and confirmed that it meets strict environmental criteria.

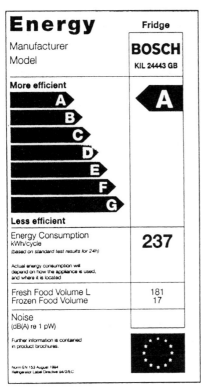

EU Energy label

Energy Efficiency
Recommended label

Eco-flower

Sinks

More time is spent at the sink than anywhere else in the kitchen. Even with the advent of dishwashers, most food preparation is undertaken in, or next to, the sink.

If possible, position the sink under or near a window to get good daylight and a view. This is also useful as the gully for the waste pipes will be on an outside wall and therefore will minimise waste pipe runs.

If there is no window, or the light and view negligible, then there is no advantage (except for shorter waste runs) in positioning a sink in front of a window and, in fact, there can be an advantage in having wall space over a sink for plate racks and storing sink utensils.

Windows behind a sink should have a cill at least 100 mm higher than the sink top to provide an upstand behind the sink, and to stop splashes dirtying the window glass.

Sink bowls should be positioned at least 400 mm away from a tall unit or return wall for elbow room.

Do not position a draining board in the 'dead' corner of an 'L'-shaped worktop as this will be inaccessible if someone is working at the sink bowl.

The question of whether it is easier to wash up from left to right or vice versa is sometimes raised. In fact it is immaterial because, in either way, the object being washed has to be picked up and passed from one hand to the other to the draining area. It might only be applicable if the draining rack is positioned over the area where the dirty dishes are put for washing. In this case, the hand which holds the brush might dictate that the opposite side should be for parking and draining. Remember, however, that both right- and left-handed people will use the sink, and that it is surprising how quickly people adapt from washing up in the opposite way to which they were accustomed.

Sinks with integral drainers and tap holes are preferable to those without as they limit the amount of water splashed on to the adjoining work surfaces. A wall-mounted mixer is also preferable to a sink-mounted mixer as it avoids lime scale and dirt accumulating around the mixer base. However, this implies making a duct behind the counter for the supply pipes which may be difficult to achieve if space is limited.

There is a wide range of sinks available, which are discussed in greater detail on pp. 76–82.

Cookers

Cookers should not be placed in corners or adjacent to a door-way where the door could swing into the cook, and people may brush past pan handles and cause accidents.

Allow at least 400 mm both sides of a cooker or a hob for worktop and elbow space.

Never position a cooker under a window where draughts could extinguish gas flames, or near flapping curtains and blinds which could catch fire.

Ideally, place the cooker or hob on an outside wall so that the fan or cooker hood can be vented directly to the outside air.

Never place wall cupboards, other than fan casings, over a hob and make sure the distance of the underside of such casings and the hob is that recommended by the fan manufacturer.

Provide a fireproof finish to act as a splash-back behind the cooker, such as tile, metal or toughened glass.

See pp. 97–106 for details of different cooking appliances.

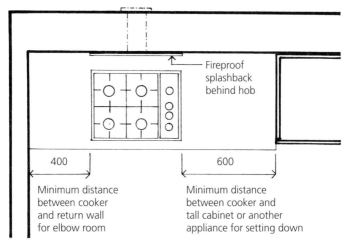

Positioning a cooker or a hob

Refrigerators and freezers

Refrigerators, which form the third part of the kitchen triangle and are therefore frequently used, are more comfortable when positioned at waist-height in a tall unit if space will allow.

Freezers are used far less frequently so, when a combination fridge/freezer is used, choose one with the refrigerator compartment on top for easier access.

Where a refrigerator or freezer is placed next to an oven provide good insulation between the two to prevent scorching and to prevent the fridge working overtime.

See pp. 125–134 for details of refrigerators and freezers.

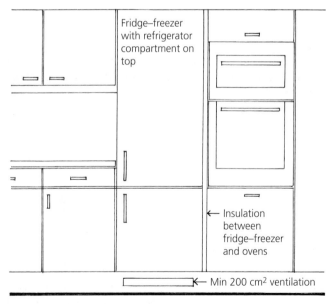

Insulation & ventilation for refrigerators & freezers

4
Kitchens for the disabled

The ambulant disabled kitchen

About 11% of the UK population is ambulant disabled. Most of these are over 50 years old and have difficulty in moving and bending down. Many are infirm and therefore need a kitchen that is well planned for their needs and to prevent accidents happening.

Planning
It is generally easier if the dining table is within the cooking area to reduce the amount of walking. If possible, provide space also for an easy chair for relaxation.

Floors should be finished with non-slip but easy to clean materials. Avoid loose mats, steps and uneven surfaces.

Skirtings with coved corner are easier to keep clean than right-angled internal corners.

Plan the sink, preparation area and cooker in one unbroken sequence. The countertop may need to be lower than the standard +900 mm, but be aware that this may inhibit the use of under-counter appliances.

Windows, particularly behind counters, should be easy to open and clean. Remote control winding gear, espagnolette bolts, pulleys and drop rods all help with stiff and inaccessible windows.

Doors should be fitted with lever handles for those with arthritic hands.

Services

Slow movers feel the cold and therefore need heating to be at least 18°C.

Good lighting is essential for safety and efficiency. Low light levels can cause fatigue and depression.

Socket outlets and switches should be positioned between +450 mm and +1200 mm above floor level.

Align light switches with door handles. Large rocker or tip switches need less pressure to operate.

The cords of ceiling switches can be fitted with large wooden rings for easier opening.

Door switches are useful for lighting the interiors of large cupboards or larders.

Electric plug tops are available with large integral handles, making plugging and unplugging easier and safer.

Appliances

Sinks with integral drainers and tap holes avoid water spilling on to counter tops.

Single lever mixer taps are easier to operate, especially for those with arthritic hands, than taps/mixers with separate round handles.

Filling large pans with water can be difficult, so position the mixer at the corner of the bowl nearest the drainer where the pan can be filled from the draining area.

Waist-high ovens, refrigerators and dishwashers are best for those who cannot easily bend down. However, note that this arrangement will take up more space.

Ovens should have drop-down doors which provide a surface on which to rest hot dishes.

Electric hobs with a continuous flat surface are safer to use than individual electric or gas rings, except in the case of the blind where gas is preferred as it can be heard.

Cabinets

Drawers, pull-out shelves and carousel trays are easier to use than fixed structures in base cupboards.

Wall storage, providing it is not too high, is useful as it reduces the need to bend down.

Open wall shelves are easier, but less dust-free, than wall cupboards with doors. Avoid wall storage in the corner of an 'L'-shaped worktop where it may be out of easy reach.

'D' handles for cabinet doors are easier to use than knobs.

For those who have difficulty walking, fix a 35 mm diameter grip rail along the front length of the worktop.

Useful devices

Many small electric appliances are extremely useful for those with limited dexterity. These include blenders, mixers, knife sharpeners, carving knives and can openers.
Similarly, electric frying pans, deep fryers, slow cookers and toasters are often preferred, and can even replace the conventional cooker.

Aids for the elderly and disabled are available from specialist manufacturers such as:

- Perching high chair with adjustable height legs
- Long-handled dustpan and brush
- 'Helping hand' device for extending reach with jaws activated by a trigger on the handle
- Kettle tipper – kettle or teapot held in tilting cradle
- Trays with non-slip finishes – also available with a raised handle for carrying with one hand
- Cutlery with easy-grip handles and angled heads

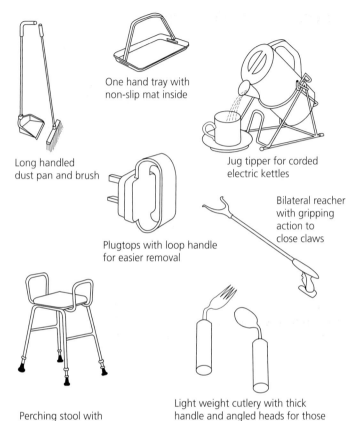

One hand tray with
non-slip mat inside

Long handled
dust pan and brush

Jug tipper for corded
electric kettles

Bilateral reacher
with gripping
action to
close claws

Plugtops with loop handle
for easier removal

Perching stool with
height adjustable legs

Light weight cutlery with thick
handle and angled heads for those
with restricted wrist movement

Kitchen aids for the disabled

Sources: *Kitchen Sense*
Spaces in the Home
Keep Able

Wheelchair user's kitchen

About 2% of the UK population use wheelchairs. Of all disabled people the wheelchair user will have most difficulty using a standard kitchen, primarily because the worktop will be too high and there will be no knee space at the sink, preparation and cooking areas.

With limited upward and forward reach, high cupboards and backs of worktops are inaccessible.

Wheelchair critical dimensions   mm

Standard wheelchair	=	1075 l × 630 w × 965 h
Top of arm rest	=	+710
Turning circle – indoor chair	=	1400
– standard chair	=	1500
– large chair	=	1700
Maximum upward reach	=	+1350
Maximum accessible shelf	=	+1300
Maximum downward reach	=	+400
Preferred worktop height	=	+800
Maximum worktop depth	=	600
Minimum knee space	=	750 w × 530 d × 660 h
Minimum cabinet toe recess	=	180 d × 200 h
(to accommodate foot rest)		

Planning

The ideal kitchen for a wheelchair user will take up more space than usual because of the need for knee space with subsequent loss of base cupboards. Also the low height of storage cupboards will reduce the amount of storage space so more cabinets will be needed.

Entrance doors from outside must have a minimum clear opening of 775 mm.
Internal doors must have a minimal clear opening of 750 mm.

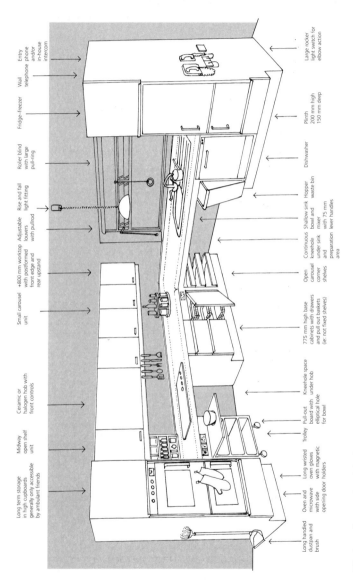

Long term storage in high cupboards generally only accessible by ambulant friends

Midway open shelf unit

Ceramic or halogen hob with front controls

Small carousel unit

+800 mm worktop with postformed front edge and rear upstand

Adjustable louvers with pullrod

Rise and fall light fitting

Roller blind with large pull-ring

Fridge-freezer

Wall telephone

Entry phone and/or in-house intercom

Oven and microwave with side opening door

Long wristed oven gloves with magnetic door holders

Trolley

Pull-out board with elliptical hole for bowl

Kneehole space under hob

775 mm high base cabinets with drawers and pull out baskets (ie: not fixed shelves)

Open carousel corner shelves

Continuous kneehole under sink and preparation area

Shallow sink bowl and mixer with 75 mm lever handles

Hopper waste bin

Dishwasher

Plinth 200 mm high 150 mm deep

Large rocker light switch for elbow action

Long handled dustpan and brush

Kitchen for a wheelchair user

Note: This distance excludes the thickness of the stop on the latch side of the door and the thickness of the open door on the hinge side.

Where possible, remove any doors to leave a clear doorway.

The dining table should be near the cooking area. Where the dining room is separate, a trolley is more convenient than a serving hatch.

Keep the sink, preparation and cooking areas in one unbroken sequence, ideally in a 'U'- or 'L'-shaped configuration. The galley kitchen is the least satisfactory type of plan, as the counters must be a minimum of 1370 mm apart for wheelchair manoeuvrability.

Floors must be level and smooth.

Windows, particularly behind counters, must be operated with remote controls such as winding gear, sash hook on pole, pulleys and drop rods.

Heating levels should be set at 18°C – ideally 20°C, particularly where doors have been removed from doorways which may create more draughts.

Sinks

Keep sinks away from corners.

The knee space should continue under the draining area as well as the preparation area alongside the bowl.

Recess the area 50 mm immediately under the counter at the sink bowl to accommodate for the chair armrests.

Sink bowls should be shallow – about 150 mm deep.

A single bowl with an integral drainer and the mixer positioned between the bowl and the drainer is the most convenient arrangement as it allows pans to be filled with water from the draining area.

For those with limited forward reach, remote controlled lever taps can be fitted to the front fascia of the sink worktop. Reduced height dishwashers are available to fit under the worktop, or in tall cabinets alongside.

Cookers

The only viable option for the wheelchair user is to have a hob with a separate oven in a tall cupboard set +400 mm above FFL.

Select a hob with the control knobs in a row at the front.

Ovens should have side hung doors for easier wheelchair access to the oven. Wire shelves within the oven should have stops to prevent them being pulled out completely.

Refrigerators

Refrigerators should not be too tall or they will be inaccessible, and should be set with the bottom at +400 mm.

A small freezing compartment at the top should be provided, unless there is a separate freezer.

Other useful devices

A pull-out worktop at +660 mm will provide another work surface which is at a better height for a wheelchair user. This worktop could include an elliptical hole 190 mm wide × 170 mm deep, lined with flexible PVC to grip a mixing bowl.

Pull-out trolleys which will fit under worktops cannot only serve as trays, but can act as another work surface or be used for eating.

Small revolving carousel shelves, for frequently used jars and condiments, can sit on the worktop.

A wall telephone and entry phone fixed at about +1000 mm.

For other useful gadgets, see pp. 47 and 48 for the ambulant disabled kitchen.

Cabinets

There are manufacturers who specialise in reduced height cabinets and appliances specifically for the wheelchair user, who also offer free advice, site surveys and drawings based on individual needs.

Base units should be fitted with drawers and pull-out baskets, rather than fixed shelves. Carousel shelves should be fitted to corner cupboards.

Variable height worktops, freestanding and wall mounted, supported on cantilevered white plastic coated steel frames are useful where kitchens are shared – as in sheltered housing or occupational therapy departments.

The height of the worktops can vary between +650 and 910 mm, operated either by a detachable winding handle or a switched electronic 24 v motor.

The standard worktop lengths are 1000 and 1500 mm, with or without sink units.

Other configurations can be manufactured to order with a maximum length of 3000 mm.

Sources: AKW Medi-care Ltd
Keep Able
N&C Phlexicare
Designing for the Disabled

5
Safety in the kitchen

Forty per cent of all the accidents in the home happen in the kitchen. Children under 5 years, and elderly people over 65, are most at risk.

Bad design and faulty maintenance are responsible for some of the risks, but most accidents are due to personal factors such as worry, temper, fatigue, haste and depression in adults, and curiosity and disobedience in children.

The kitchen should have a first aid box or cabinet which should be lockable or kept well out of reach of small children.

Planning

The safest layouts are those where the cooker, work surface and sink are in an unbroken sequence, uninterrupted by doorways. This avoids carrying hot dishes and boiling pans across circulation spaces.

Never position cookers near a window where draughts can extinguish gas flames and where curtains or blinds might catch fire.

Check that fan casings and cooker hoods are positioned according to the manufacturers' recommendations, which must be well above a hob or a high level gas grill. See p. 118.

Drying racks should never be placed over cookers as towels may fall down and catch fire.

All appliances and sinks should be kept well away from inward opening doors, which may bang into the person using them.

A worktop area should be provided both sides of a cooker and should be level with the hob surround. Pan handles should always be parked sideways, out of the reach of small children.

Climbing up on rickety chairs to reach things accounts for many accidents, particularly amongst the elderly who should be provided with a small stepladder or a *kick-step*.

Good lighting of working areas is essential to prevent cuts, burns, scalds and fingers being trapped in moving parts.

Floors must be level, with no steps or raised thresholds, and the finish should be non-slip. Avoid wax polishes which can be slippery when wet. Water, and particularly grease and oil spills, should be mopped up as soon as they occur.

Lack of storage will result in things being left on the floor – such as shopping bags over which people can trip.

Children

Young children should not be allowed to play in the kitchen where their mother can trip over their toys while she is handling boiling pans or sharp knives. Cooks' knives are best hung on magnetic racks rather than drawers which can be accessible to young fingers.

Toddlers must also be prevented from eating and drinking pets' food and water, and putting polythene bags over their heads which can cause swift suffocation.

Bleach, and other household poisons, should be stored in cupboards above worktop level so as to be out of children's reach.

Electrical appliances – safety aspects

A kitchen must be provided with at least four socket outlets above the worktop to cope with small electrical appliances such as a kettle, food processor, coffee machine and toaster. Where there are inadequate sockets, trailing flexes will result. Twin socket outlets are preferable to single sockets as these will discourage the use of adaptors and consequent overloading of circuits.

Sockets and spur switches must be positioned well away from sink units to reduce the risk of handling with wet hands. They should also not be placed behind hobs, where arms could be burned and sleeves catch fire when reaching over a live burner.

Large appliances built into cabinets have spur switches above the worktop, connected to socket outlets behind the appliances, so that they can be remotely controlled and also be pulled out for servicing.

Gas cookers – safety aspects

Gas cookers are safer if they have automatic ignition, as the burners will light if a child accidentally turns on a control. Some cookers also have automatic re-ignition which re-lights the burner should the flame be accidentally extinguished.

Dealing with fire

Fat catching fire in a pan is one of the most common causes of kitchen fires.

Water should never be poured on to flaming fat as this will spread the flame in an instant.

A fire blanket or an aerosol fire extinguisher should be used to smother the flames and then the burner should be switched off. Failing that, a damp cloth can be draped over the pan to cut off the air, and left in position until cool.

Aerosol cans will explode if they get too hot, and should be stored in a cool place.

1 Everyday food out of easy reach
2 Cloth drying over hob could fall and catch fire
3 Cupboard door left open could bang someone's head
4 Hob too near open window – curtains could catch fire
5 Socket too near sink and is overloaded with flex trailing behind sink
6 Aerosol bomb could explode from heat from hob
7 Kettle is playing steam over electric socket
8 Cat is going to walk over food preparation worktop
9 Drawer full of sharp knives left open to child
10 Poisonous substances accessible to child
11 Saucepan handle left sticking out for child to reach
12 Shopping bag left about on floor – could cause fall
13 Spilt liquid not mopped up making floor slippery
14 Cat's food left accessible to child
15 Unstuck down tile could trip someone up

Disaster kitchen

Smoke alarms

Smoke alarms are required by the Building Regulations in all dwellings.

Summarised below are the requirements which pertain to domestic kitchens:

If a dwelling does **NOT** have an automatic fire detection and alarm system, then a suitable number of smoke alarms must be provided. They must be *mains operated* and may have a secondary battery operated power supply.

There must be at least one *smoke alarm* on each floor. They should be *linked* so that the alarm signal operates in all locations.
They should be sited so that is there is a smoke alarm in the circulation space within 7.5 m of every habitable room.

Where a *kitchen area* is **NOT** separated from a stairway or circulation space by a door, there should be a compatible interlinked *heat detector* in the kitchen, in addition to whatever smoke alarms are needed in the circulation spaces.

Smoke alarms should be *ceiling mounted* and at least 300 mm from walls and light fittings.
They may also be *wall mounted* provided they are above the level of any doorways opening into the space.

Smoke alarms must be easily *accessible* for maintenance, testing and cleaning.

Smoke alarms should **NOT** be fixed in *cooking areas* where steam, condensation or fumes could give false alarms.

Source: Building Regulations – Approved Document B

6
Services

Water supply

All water fittings and their installation should conform to WRAS (*Water Regulation Advisory Scheme*).
This is an organisation which provides guidance to the *Water Supply (water fittings) Regulations 1999.*
These regulations have superseded the former *Water Byelaws* issued by individual water companies.

Installation of water fittings should be undertaken by members of a recognised trade association, such as the Institute of Plumbing.

Pipework must be readily accessible, not chased into plaster or in floor ducts under cabinets. Make sure that stop cocks which should be provided under sinks, before dishwashers and any other appliances with water supplies, are reasonably accessible.

Where a sink waste discharges over a gully outside, this is a good place to incorporate a branch for a hose union tap, set about 600 mm high for garden use. The tap must be fitted with double check valves and be isolated by an inside stop cock to prevent freezing in winter.

Sinks are best fitted with 75 mm deep seal *bottle traps* which are easy to undo should anything unintended fall down the waste.

Hot water for sinks can either be supplied by a central storage cylinder or, where pipe runs are long, by a separate under-counter 'point-of-use' electric water heater. However, where dishwashers and washing machines are plumbed-in nearby, it is generally more energy efficient to connect them to both hot and cold supplies as the programme time will be reduced. However, in this case, the water supplied should not exceed 60°C.

Water treatment

Approximately 60% of the UK is supplied with *hard water*. The resulting limescale build-up on heating elements can considerably reduce heating and hot water efficiency. Corrosion can

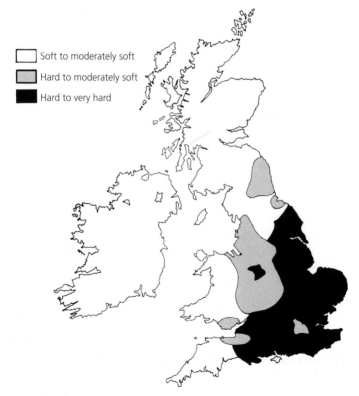

Water hardness

occur beneath the scale, reducing life expectancy and scale particles will clog shower heads and mixer outlets, reducing flow and proper mixing of hot and cold water. It will also leave unsightly, but not harmful, limescale deposits round tap bases, plug holes, and water marks on stainless steel sinks and metal implements.

The hardness of the water can be obtained from the water company. It is usually classified as soft: 0–50 ppm (parts per million) to very hard: over 300 ppm.

The hardness is determined by the geology of the ground through which the rainwater runs. Water will pick up calcium or magnesium from chalk or limestone, but not if it passes through granite or peaty soils.

Soft water can pick up trace metals from pipework which may eventually cause leaking pipes and corrode copper cylinders.

Water softeners

Water softeners consist of a resin cylinder which is filled with sodium chloride (salt). They are plumbed into the cold mains supply inside the house. As water passes through the cylinder, calcium and magnesium are removed and are replaced by sodium salts.

Water softeners are usually fully automatic and only need periodic filling with salt.

They take up space typically about $300 \times 450 \times 800$ mmh and need a drain connection for the hose waste and an electricity supply for a time clock.

Water softeners should be fitted after the mains supply of water to any drinking water taps because the taste of softened water is unpleasant and is not good for brewing tea. There is also some evidence that drinking soft water can aggravate heart conditions and may be unsuitable for people who require a low sodium diet.

Scale inhibitors

Scale inhibitors present a far cheaper alternative to dealing with limescale, but opinions vary as to how effective they really are. The difference between scale inhibitors and water softeners is that they break up the limescale and leave it in suspension, rather than eliminating it altogether.

This is done by passing the mains water through powerful magnets which alter the structure of the hard water salts, or by electrolysis where the water passes through a copper cathode and a zinc anode which creates a mild electric current, leaving the limescale in suspension rather than clinging to the surface of the pipes. Some scale inhibitors involve polyphosphate dosing whereby a very small amount of a compound of sodium, calcium, phosphorus and oxygen is added to the water, either in the form of small containers hung in an expansion tank feeding the hot water system, or by a chemical cartridge plumbed into the pipework. Both methods require the chemicals to be replaced every six months.

It is thought that scale inhibitors are more effective where a large volume of water is used on a frequent basis, as it is the action of the running water which promotes the action. They have the virtue of taking up very little room – typically 150–200 mm length of pipe run and are maintenance free. They have a typical life expectancy of at least 10 years.

Filtered drinking water

According to the Drinking Water Inspectorate, drinking water quality in the UK is improving with 98.95% of 2.9 million tests meeting EU standards. However, some people worry about the smell of chlorine, sediments and rust particles affecting taste and prefer to have their water filtered.

There are various jug devices on the market but if a plumbed in solution is required, under-sink cartridges can be fixed into the mains water supply pipe before entering the sink mixer. Cartridges/filters generally need renewing every six months. See p. 85 for filtered water mixers.

Boiling and chilled water on tap

There are over-sink and under-sink water heaters which can provide boiling water and some can also provide chilled water. It is claimed that they use less electricity than a jug kettle and have the advantage over a kettle of not cluttering the work-top as they are connected to a dual-control tap over the sink.

Sources: WRAS and Salamander Engineering Ltd

Gas supply

Gas pipes should be accessible for leak detection, suspended on clips away from the wall surface and encased in sleeves where passed through walls. They should not touch hot water pipes or electric cables.

Stop cocks should be provided before each appliance and connected to cookers, ovens and hobs with flexible hoses to enable them to be pulled out for servicing.

Where no mains gas is available and gas is the preferred fuel for cooking, this can be provided in the form of propane gas cylinders. This gas has a higher calorific value than mains gas and can therefore be connected to appliances with small bore pipework.

As the propane gas is under pressure, the containers should be positioned outside the house, in free air, away from any heat sources. It is usual to provide twice the number of cylinders required, which allows half to be in use and the other half to be in reserve. This allows time for the empty cylinders to be renewed by the local supplier.

Electrical wiring

All wiring should be in accordance with the current Wiring Regulations issued by the Institution of Electrical Engineers (IEE). It is advisable to use electrical contractors approved by the National Inspection Council for Electrical Installation Contracting (NICEIC).

Above the *worktop*, socket outlets will be needed for the following typical appliances: kettle, blender, food processor. These are likely to be permanently sitting on the worktop. In addition there may be more occasionally used items such as: whisk, juice extractor, coffee mill, tin opener, etc.

At the *cooking area*, sockets may be needed for an electric frying pan and hand-held tools, like a whisk or blender which are used directly into saucepans on the hob.

At the *serving area*, sockets may be needed for: toaster, carving knife, warming hot plate.

All sockets should be twin sockets to save space and to discourage the use of adapters.

Note that an electric kettle can have a rating as high as 3 kW. It is therefore important that the socket outlet likely to be used for this is not on the same ring main as a major appliance.

Spur boxes or unswitched socket outlets for appliances not exceeding 3 kW should be provided behind large appliances and connected to switches above the worktop for: dishwasher, waste disposer, water heater/chiller, extractor fan/cooker hood, refrigerator, freezer, fridge-freezer.

Major cooking appliances will need a separate circuit to cope with the high voltage of electric cookers, ovens and hobs, connected to a consumer unit or switch of appropriate watt rating. Saving energy should be considered when specifying cooking appliances, as their wattage can vary considerably.

Lighting

Good lighting in kitchens is an essential pre-requisite. Inadequate lighting can cause accidents, fatigue and lead to bad hygiene. During daylight hours there may be sufficient light, but this will vary according to the size and orientation of the window, the season and time of day.

Worktop lighting

The main source of artificial light is needed for the worktops. This can best be achieved by mounting light fittings behind battens fixed to the front edge of wall cupboards.

There are several types of *linear* light fittings suitable for use under wall cabinets such as the following:

Small diameter fluorescent tubes with electronic ballast for instant start fitted with 8 W and 13 W warm-white lamps. This is the most economic option as the tubes have a very long life. They also have the advantage of giving off relatively little heat.

Low voltage fittings with two, three or four 10 or 12 W halogen capsule lamps fitted into linear rectangular section tubes with integral transformers.
These lamps give a bright white light and are reasonably long lasting.

'Architectural' tungsten 35, 60 and 120 watt striplights in three different lengths.
Elegant in appearance with a warm coloured light, but lamps are short lived so are not popular as they are hideously expensive to replace.

Source: Mr Resistor

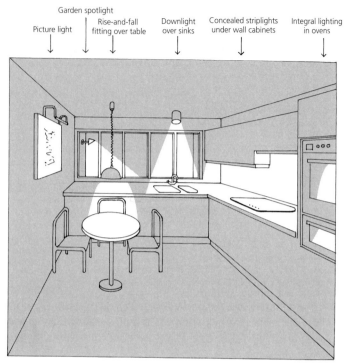

Garden spotlight
Picture light | Rise-and-fall fitting over table | Downlight over sinks | Concealed striplights under wall cabinets | Integral lighting in ovens

Kitchen lighting

General lighting

Where there are no wall cupboards, such as over a sink in front of a window, then a downlighter, directional spotlight or shaded pendant light can be fixed to the ceiling.

Ovens, cooker hoods and refrigerators usually have their own interior lights to aid visual recognition and promote hygiene by showing up dirt.

General lighting can also be provided by lights fixed above cupboards or at high level on walls to illuminate the ceiling. Alternatively, several individual low voltage spotlights can be recessed into the ceiling, or into cabinet plinths to light the floor.

LV stainless steel triangular light
with 10/20 W halogen lamps
by Hettich

LV light for mounting under
glass shelves with 10 W halogen capsule lamp – by Hettich

LV brushed nickel fitting with integral transformer
and 4 × 20 W halogen capsule lamps
by JCC Lighting

Energy saving fluorescent lamps
housed in aluminium body with white
perspex diffuser and integral switch
with 2 × 9 W tubes – by Häfele

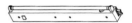

Standard fluorescent strip-
light with rocker switch for
6 W, 8 W and 13 W tubes
by Häfele

Aluminium reflector with polycarbonate diffuser
25 mm × 25 mm for 6 W, 8 W, 11 W and 13 W
fluorescent tubes – by Light Graphix

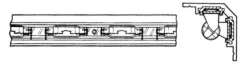

LV linear festoon system with 5 W or 10 W lamps
mounted on integral transformer in rigid housing in
any length up to 3 m max. – by Light Graphix

Worktop illumination

Wall washer with 100/150 W linear
TH lamp – by John Cullen

LV fully recessed sealed glass down
lighter for wet areas with 20–50 W
dichroic lamps – by John Cullen

External die-cast aluminium
spotlight with 150 TH linear
lamp – by Contract Lighting

LV chrome picture light with
2 × 20 W capsule lamps
by JCC Lighting

Picture light in polished chrome
with 8 W, 11 W or 13 W
fluorescent tubes
by Light Graphix

White rise-and-fall fitting with max
100 W lamp – by First light

General illumination

Dining tables can be lit with rise-and-fall pendant lights which
are best connected to a plug-in ceiling rose so that the fitting
can be completely removed if the table is moved to the wall
for a large party.

Where there is an adjacent garden which is fully visible from the dining area, external spotlights can illuminate it at night making it possible to light the dining table solely with candles.

Heating

In the kitchen, high ambient temperatures are gained from cooking so, except for a dining/kitchen room, heating levels need not be as high as for other living spaces.
As wall space is at a premium there is seldom room to fit a conventional radiator but there are other forms of heating which may be considered.

Underfloor heating

Underfloor heating is one of the more convenient ways of heating kitchens as it leaves the walls entirely free for cabinets and appliances. The disadvantage is its slow response time to heat up and cool down.
There are various types: hot water pipes, warm air ducts and electric cables.

The most recent advance has been electric mats embedded with such small diameter heating cables that the overall thickness is no more than 3 mm. These can be laid within the thickness of the bedding mortar under stone or ceramic tiles. This is therefore particularly suitable for installing in existing buildings as it barely raises the finished floor level.
Typical rating is 125 watts/m^2 with sizes up to 15 m^2.

For small kitchens, there are also mats with low voltage flexible heating elements encapsulated in a 2 mm thick polyester sheet which provide safe and cheap background heating.
Typical panel is 600 × 500 mm with ratings of:
24 watts @ 24 volts and 33 watts @ 28 volts.

Kickspace heaters

These are small fan convector heating units designed to be fitted into the plinth board below base cupboards.

The plinth board must be a minimum 140 mm high and recessed no more than 75 mm.

There are two basic types: all electric models or those which can be connected to central heating pipework.

Outputs range from 1–2 kW.

Typically they measure about 500 w × 400 d × 100 h (mm). During summer months the fan-only option can be used to circulate air.

Low voltage models are also available for use in wet areas.

Wall-mounted fan heaters

Compact heaters with a downward flow of hot air.

They have a fast warm-up time and are rated at 2 kW with a splash-roof protection rating of IPX4.

Typical size is about 250 w × 250 h × 110 d (mm).

They are normally operated with a pull cord and some incorporate an energy-saving thermostat.

While efficient and space saving, the noise of the fan can be irritating.

Infra-red heaters

Radiant electric wall heaters with elements encased in silica or ceramic sleeves, with ratings of 0.5 to 1.8 kW and a spray-proof protection rating of IPX3. Mounted at high level, they provide rapid, silent warmth which can be beamed down at angles from 20°–40°.

Towel radiators

Ladder-type towel radiators in enamel, stainless steel or chrome finishes. Designed primarily for bathrooms they can also be useful for kitchens where the larger models can provide full heating and smaller models provide a place to hang and dry towels.

Ratings from 150–1700 W.
Sizes from: 500–750 w, 90–150 d and 650–1800 h (mm).

Sources: Enerfoil
Myson
Dimplex
Zehnder

High level wall-hung infra-red heater
by Dimplex

Wall hung fan convector
heater – by Dimplex

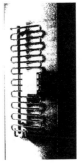

Cobra-Therm towel
radiator – by Bisque

Kickspace convector heater
by Myson

Low voltage panel heater for bedding in
ceramic floor tile adhesive – by Enerfoil

Heaters – other than conventional radiators

Ventilation

Good ventilation is essential in a kitchen, not only to extract heat, steam and fumes from cooking, but to satisfy the Building Regulations as set out below.

Building Regulations

An extractor fan or cooker hood is a mandatory requirement:

TYPE OF KITCHEN	BACKGROND VENTILATION	MECHANICAL VENTILATION
kitchens with opening windows (no minimum size)	4000 mm^2	30 litres/second adjacent to hob* **OR** 60 litres/second elsewhere **OR** passive stack ventilation (PSV) to BRE information paper 13/94 **OR** with appropriate third party certification such as a BBA certificate
kitchens without natural light	air inlet such as 10 mm gap under door	extract fan as above with 15 minute over-run with fan operated by light switch

*When incorporated within a cooker hood **OR** when located near the ceiling within 300 mm of the centreline of the hob and under humidistat control.

Where there is an open flue within the same room as an extract or fan, difficulties can occur – such as the fan drawing noxious flue gases into the room. If the following conditions can be met, the need for an extractor fan may be dispensed with:

Where there is a *solid fuel* open-flued appliance that is the primary source of heating, cooking or water heating

OR

Where the appliance is burning *other fuels*, it is required that: the appliance has a flue with a free area at least 125 mm diameter

AND

the appliance has combustion and dilution air inlets which are permanently open when not in use so that the ventilation path is unrestricted (i.e. no dampers).

With flued *gas* appliances which are located in a kitchen where a fan is desired – it has been found that an extract rate of not more than 20 litres/second will be unlikely to cause spillage of gases, although it will be necessary to carry out a spillage test in accordance with BS 54440: part 1, clause 4.3.2.3.

Advice on the construction of *oil-fired* appliances is contained in Technical Information Note T1/112 from OFTEC
(Oil firing technical association for the petroleum Industry).

Where kitchens are combined with a *habitable* room such as in a kitchen/dining room, the provisions for ventilation need not be duplicated provided the greatest provision for rapid, background and mechanical ventilation is made.

A habitable room must have an opening window of at least 1/20th of the floor area **AND**
background ventilation of at least 8000 mm^2.
Note that for the purposes of ventilation in the Building Regulations a kitchen is not considered a habitable room.

Source: *Approved document F, the Building Regulations 1995*

Communications

As the hub of the household, where so much time is spent, it is important to consider installing in the kitchen some of the following forms of communication.

Notice board
At its simplest, a board made of cork or softboard with drawing pins or a metallic sheet with magnets for messages, shopping lists, reminders, family photos, postcards, etc.

Telephone
A wall-hung telephone extension or pocket for a mobile phone with adjacent note pad and pen.

Entry phone
Where the kitchen is far from the front door, an entry phone system is useful.

Baby alarm
Essential for new babies – either simple battery operated or by closed circuit TV.

Desk
Where space allows, a small desk top or piece of counter with knee space for a stool is much appreciated by serious cooks for studying and writing recipes, paying bills, sorting post, etc.

Radio and TV

There are some small format combinations of radio, television, CD and DVD players designed specifically for kitchen use, which can be mounted under kitchen wall cabinets. Some can even be wall fixed.

Televisions should be kept away from direct sources of heat and moisture, and the screens out of the path of direct sunlight.

Television, radio, DVD and CD players, internet browser and key board for mounting under wall cabinets – by Kitchenvision

Television with 15″ swivelling screen in SS frame to suit 500 and 600 mm wide tall cupboards – by Kitchenvision

LCD television and radio – by Häfele

Mounted under wall cabinets, screen folds up when not in use

Wall mounted

Kitchen radio/ TV/CD players

7
Sinks and mixers

Of all appliances, the sink is the workhorse of the kitchen. Research shows that about 60% of the time spent in the kitchen is at the sink, compared with about 20% at the cooker. For this reason alone, it is important that the right sink is chosen at the outset.

The sink is also the least likely appliance to be replaced, partly because of the expense of altering the plumbing but mostly because it will affect the worktop in which it sits, where the cut-out hole will almost certainly be different or the bowl(s) may be an integral part of the worktop material.

For locating the sink within the kitchen, see pp. 41, 42.

A single sink bowl is not enough for washing food, filling pans, disposing of waste, hand washing dishes and/or clothes, doing flowers, etc. Ideally houses have a separate utility/laundry room with a large deep sink for laundry which can also deal with washing muddy boots, soaking clothes and filling vases.

Even in the smallest kitchen a '$1\frac{1}{2}$ bowl sink' is preferable to a single sink bowl as it allows for slops to be disposed of in the smaller sink.

In seriously small kitchens, where there is room for only a single bowl, choose the largest possible so that a smaller washing up bowl may be used within the sink, leaving space around for rinsing dishes or disposing of waste.

The small kitchen may also benefit from a chopping board accessory designed to fit over the sink bowl which will extend the available worktop area when the bowl is not in use.

Types of sinks

Sinks come in the following broad categories:

Inset	a sink top inserted into a hole cut out of the worktop and secured with a self-rimming flange.
Sit-on	sink top designed to fit over a specific sized base cupboard which will butt up against adjoining worktop surfaces and leave an undesirable dirt-trapping slot.
Under-mounted	individual or double bowl units fixed to the underside of work tops made of solid material.
Integral with worktop	bowls cast or welded to a worktop of the same material, i.e. composite stone, Corian, SS, etc.
Individual	individual bowl(s) such as the traditional fireclay Belfast sink which can sit on or be adjacent to worktops or draining boards.

Sink unit surrounds should include holes for mixers to contain water splashes and keep limescale spotting off the adjacent worktop. Ideally sink mixers should be *wall mounted* to avoid the problem of scale and dirt accumulating round the base of mixers. But this involves making a duct behind the sink to accommodate pipework and to allow the underside of the spout to project about 110 mm over the sink top.

Waste outlets are better positioned at the rear of the sink bowl to allow more flat area as a work surface. This prevents plugs from being accidentally removed and makes for more accessible storage space in the cupboard underneath the bowl.

Note that the depths of sinks can vary from as shallow as 120 mm to as deep as 250 mm.

Building Regulations require a minimum 40 mm trap with 75 mm depth of seal for sinks. In practice it is best for all sink wastes to be fitted with *bottle traps* so that blockages and lost jewellery can be more easily removed, but note that waste disposers must NOT be fitted to a bottle trap. See p. 95.

A good feature found in some adjacent sinks is a slight indent in the dividing wall between the sinks which will divert water overflowing from one full bowl into the other.

Beware 'universal' configuration of sink and draining boards. These are sink units which have a tap hole punched in both sides of the unit, allowing the unit to be handed as required. This results in the unused tap hole being filled with a blank, causing an obstruction around which dirt will collect. More expensive ranges have the option of RH or LH drainers which avoid this problem.

Sink accessories

Sinks are often supplied with optional *accessories* such as:

mixer tap
plumbing set, i.e. wastes, linking pipework and trap
drainer basket
draining trays
strainer bowl – a colander generally for smaller sink
chopping board – hardwood, to fit larger bowl

Some or all of these may be included in the package price. Check that the mixer, in particular, is the model required and whether the client needs the accessories and will have enough cupboard space to store them.

Stainless steel sinks

Stainless steel is still the prime choice for kitchen sinks.

It is virtually indestructible, rustless, seamless and non-porous, so is hygienic and continues to look good after many years of hard use. The resilient properties of the sheet material soften impact blows.
The only products known to dull the metal are very strong bleaches and silver dipping liquid.
The recommended composition of the material is:
18/8 nickel/chrome content (18/10 is better) to BS 1449 Part 2 and Euronorm 88.71, grade 304 with thicknesses ranging from 0.9 to 1.5 mm.
The underside of bowls should be applied with sound-deadening panels or a material such as bituminous rubber compound to minimise drumming.

In hard water areas, limescale spots will show up on stainless steel. These cause no harm and can be removed easily with vinegar or proprietary limescale removing liquids.

The finish is usually polished but, at slight extra cost, linen, brushed and satin finishes are available for the surrounds and draining boards. These will help to disguise limescale spotting and fine scratches, although the normal polished finish will acquire a 'brushed' look in time anyway so these finishes are somewhat questionable.

Stainless steel sink bowls can also be welded on to *stainless steel worktops*. See p. 166.

Stainless steel sinks are available in many configurations:

single round bowl	inset or undermounted
single rectangular bowl	inset or undermounted
double rectangular bowls	inset or undermounted
single bowl with drainer(s)	inset or sit-on
double bowls with drainer(s)	inset or sit-on
corner bowl(s) with drainer(s)	inset

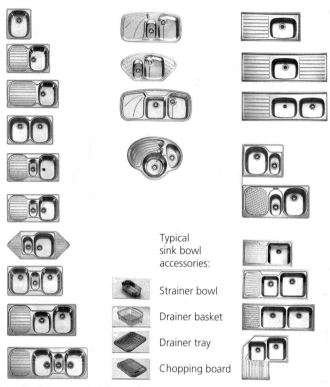

Typical
sink bowl
accessories:

Strainer bowl

Drainer basket

Drainer tray

Chopping board

Inset stainless steel sinks and accessories by Franke

Brass sinks

This is a limited range of individual sinks and inset bowls with drainers available in brass. Inevitably they tarnish and the manufacturers recommend 'cleaning on a daily basis with a water soluble cleaner'. This should deter most clients except for those with a fleet of servants.

Plastic sinks

Plastic sinks are made of polypropylene or other polymers. They can stain and are not as heat resistant as other sink materials. They tend to be used in economy installations and carry only a limited guarantee.

Solid surface sinks

These are sinks made of silica, recycled glass, quartz or other stone particles bound in a matrix of tough acrylic resins with various proprietary names generally ending in 'ite' as they come in granite-like colours ranging from nearly white in tone to nearly black.

They claim to be strong, durable, resistant to impact, scalding, staining, and are heat resistant to 180°C. The quality of individual makes may be judged by the guarantees which range from 10 to 20 years.
Despite claims of indestructibility, manufacturers advise never to use undiluted bleach on the surface.

Ceramic sinks

Made of glazed fireclay, ceramic sinks are heavy and thick in profile. They have a hard, non-porous surface giving good resistance to detergents, abrasive acids, alkalis, hot and cold temperatures. The glaze has a shiny bleachable, hygienic appearance is generally white in colour, but it will chip if subject to heavy blows.

They are available in standard inset bowl and drainer patterns and also as so-called *Butler sinks* with deep rectangular single or double bowls and in traditional *Belfast* shapes.

Ceramic sinks can be set under solid material worktops, often with the deep front side exposed to view. These sinks are heavy and need substantial support.

Under-mounted sink bowls – by Carron

Ceramic sink with rear shelf which can be punched for mixer tap by Villeroy & Boch

L-shaped solid surface sink unit for a corner situation – by Carron

'Waterstation' with revolving top bulit into a corner or free-standing by B&L Rieber

Sit-on SS sink unit – by Carron

Different types of kitchen sink

Sink taps and mixers

Brassware for sinks has developed into an art form of its own, very often with price tags to match. It is not unusual for the mixer to cost considerably more than the sink.

Historically, the kitchen sink had two high-necked *pillar taps,* from which the *mixer valve* or *combination tap* was developed, usually in the form of a *bridge mixer* with pillar taps mounted on adjustable unions so as to fit variable centre line dimensions of pre-drilled tap holes.

Eventually two tap holes were standardised at 180 mm centres so the more elegant *deck mixer* appeared.
All these patterns are still available which is useful for replacing existing fittings.

From this 'two tap-hole' situation came the *monobloc* mixer with a single body, a single spout and two tap handles on either side.

About the same time, *ceramic disc* operation was developed which has several advantages over the traditional *screw-down* (or *compression*) handles as they have the benefit of a quick quarter-turn for full flow, need no washer replacement and have a long working life.

Then the monobloc ceramic disc *single lever mixer* emerged which is the most efficient type as it requires only one hand to operate and it saves water as a single quick downward action is all that is needed to shut off the water supply.

Mixers with cross top or round handles have screw-down operation while mixers with ceramic discs have various forms of lever handles.

Pillar taps

Bridge mixer

Deck mixer

Monoblock mixer

Single lever mixer

Evolution of the tap mixer shown here with current models by Ideal Standard

Filtered water mixers

There are monobloc single lever mixers which supply filtered cold water from a cartridge housed in the cabinet under the sink (see also p. 62).

Note that some models require minimum 3 or 5 bar water pressure.
These are available in various patterns such as:

- monobloc mixer with three handles for hot, cold and filtered water.
- monobloc mixer with two handles, where the cold handle is turned in the opposite direction for filtered water.
- monobloc mixer with two independently rotating spouts, with one handle for hot and cold water and the other for filtered water.
- single lever mixer where the lever is turned in an anti-clockwise direction for filtered water.

Rinsing spray attachment

Several mixers have provision for a separate *rinsing spray* or *hand spray* attached to a flexible hose which sits alongside the mixer in a separate tap hole.

There are also mixers with a rinsing spray which pulls out of the mixer spout.
The ultimate version of this type is the so-called *'professional'* or *'chef's'* deck mixer which has a long adjustable spring balanced powerful rinsing spray designed to rinse and wash both inside AND outside the sink bowl if required.
Note that this type of mixer generally requires minimum 5 or even 7 bar water pressure.

'Professional' mixer with spring balanced long powerful spray attachment by Blanco

'Semi-professional' mixer with height adjustable hand-set – by Blanco

Mono block mixer with 500 mm pull-out spray by Astracast

Single lever mixer with pull-out spray by Hansgrohe

Single lever mixer for filtered coldwater by Ideal Standard

Single lever mixer for filtered cold water by Astracast

Hydrotap delivers both boiling and chilled filtered water from an under-sink heater and chiller by Zip

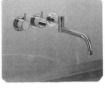

Three hole sink mixer by Ideal Standard

Wall-mounted single handle mixer with swivel spout-by Vola

Wall-mounted two handle mixer with swivel spout-by Vola

Sink mixers

Tap holes

Tap holes can be a problem, first and foremost because limescale and grime gathers round the tap base.

It is far better to install a *wall-mounted mixer* leaving the sink-top or countertop free of holes. Unfortunately there are not many wall-mounted models available and accommodating a duct behind the counter is not always possible.

Tap holes in metal sinktops tend to be pre-drilled and it is not always possible to get the desired sink pattern with the right number of holes. This may result is having to use a blank, hand-rinse or soap dispenser to fill an unwanted hole. Sink bowls mounted under solid surface or stone countertops get over this problem as tap holes can be drilled as required.

Tap construction

Most mixers are *dual flow* where hot and cold water is separated within the spout and is only mixed at the spout outlet. This is to avoid the possibility of *backflow* which might contaminate the mains cold water supply.

Where *single flow* mixers are installed, they must be fitted with *double check valves* to conform to WRAS requirements.

Check that mixers specified will operate with the available water pressure. Models can vary from needing a minimum of 0.2 bar up to 0.7 bar (roughly 2 m up to 7 m head of water).

Sink taps are made of brass and come with various finishes:

bright chrome	bronze
satin chrome	brushed nickel
brushed steel	gold plate
polished brass	epoxy powder-coated colours

Sources: Astracast, BGL Rieber, Blanco, Carron, Franke, Hansgrohe, Ideal-Standard, Villeroy & Boch, Vola, Zip

8
Waste disposal

More household waste is generated in the kitchen than any other room. Most is produced near the sink and dishwasher which is the logical place to position waste bins.

Recycling waste

A good deal of waste can be recycled.
Many local authorities will collect the following items providing it is clean and separated for recycling:

glass, aluminium and tin cans, paper and also plastic containers if they are marked with the triangular recycle logo.

For households with a garden, organic waste can be put on a *compost heap.* This can include all vegetable waste, egg shells, tea bags, etc., but should NOT include bread, meat or fat which will encourage rats.

'Mobious Loop'
a recycling logo
in general use

Recycling logo from DEFRA
(Dept. for Environment Food
and Rural Affairs) with different coloured grounds for
different types of waste

PETE
Polyethylene
terepthalate

HDPE
High density
polyethylene

V
Polyvinyl
chloride

LDPE
Low density
polyethylene

PP
Polypropylene

PS
Polystyrene

OTHER
All other resins
and multi materials

Recycling logos for plastic materials

Waste bins

In an ideal world, kitchen waste would be separated into six bins as follows:

vegetables, teabags, eggshells	for compost heap
metal cans	for recycling
glass	for recycling
plastic	for recycling
paper	for recycling
anything else	for dustbin

This is obviously difficult to achieve especially when space is at a premium.

However, even the smallest kitchen should have at least three bins: one for general rubbish and two for metal and glass.

There are various proprietary systems for fitting waste bins into cabinets such as:

Pull-out rectangular bins suspended on runners with combinations of two, three and five bins, depending on cabinet width.

Bins fitted to insides of doors with lids opening automatically as doors are opened.

Tall bins to fit 300 mm wide cabinets with pull-out or hopper doors.

20 litre SS round bin
for side-hung door and
400 mm wide cabinet
by Häfele

19 litre pull-out
plastic bin for min.
300 mm wide
cabinet
by Isaac Lord

16 litre total capacity
for two compartments
in SS bin for side-hung
door and min 450 wide
cabinet – by Häfele

50 litre total in 3 bins
and 2 baskets for pull-
out door to 500 mm
wide cabinet – by Häfele

30 litre total
in three SS
bins for pull-
out door and
min. 400 mm
wide cabinet
by Issac Lord

32 litre total in
three SS bins
for pull-out
door and min.
500 W cabinet
by Issac Lord

30 litre bin front-fixed
to door with tilting
mechanism for
500 mm wide cabinet
by Häfele

Wastebins

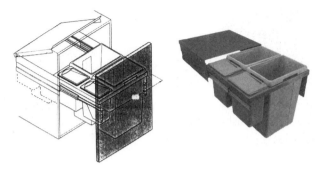

87 litres total in 2 × 35 litre bins and 2 × 8.5 litre bins hung on sides of 600 mm cabinet – by Häfele

 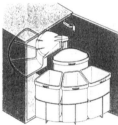

39 litres total in 1 × 12 litre bin and 3 × 9 litre bins fixed to side and base of 500 mm wide cabinet by Häfele

15 litre (or 11 litre) plastic bin and SS lid fixed into work-top with soft rubber ring housed into SS ring which trims hole in worktop by Isaac Lord

Dustbins

Ideally, dustbins should be on the same level as the kitchen, with covered access not more than 18 m from the kitchen and 50 m from dustcart access.

For homes with solid fuel appliances, a metal dustbin will be needed for hot ashes.

In the same area, separate bins could be arranged to store glass, plastic and paper to be collected for recycling.

Waste disposers

For households with a garden and a compost heap, a waste disposer in the kitchen may not be required.

Otherwise the arguments for waste disposers are as follows:

- useful in multi-storey flats where storage and collection of waste is a problem
- eliminates handling of wet leftover food
- prevents smells as food is flushed away promptly
- more hygienic as rotting food in bins encourages smells, bacteria, insects and rodents
- reduces the amount of waste that ends in landfill sites
- resulting sludge at water treatment plants can be recycled into soil conditioner.

Arguments against waste disposers are:

- only deals with 15% of total household rubbish
- uses 9 litres of water per head per day so will add to water bills
- increases sludge in sewers.

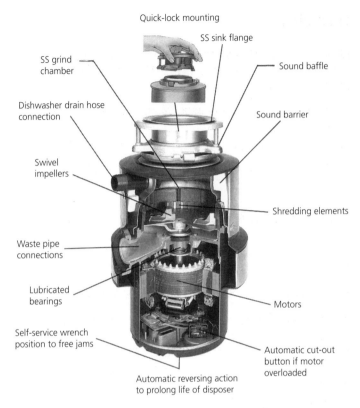

Quick-lock mounting

SS sink flange

SS grind chamber

Sound baffle

Dishwasher drain hose connection

Sound barrier

Swivel impellers

Shredding elements

Waste pipe connections

Lubricated bearings

Motors

Self-service wrench position to free jams

Automatic cut-out button if motor overloaded

Automatic reversing action to prolong life of disposer

Continuous feed waste disposer – by In-Sink-Erator

Models

There are two types of waste disposer:

continuous feed   turn on cold water tap, switch on and push food through sink waste under running water

batch feed   place waste in unit, insert plug which seals unit, run water and turn plug to activate motor

Continuous feed models are more convenient to use especially when there is a great deal of waste.

Batch feed models are safer as it is not possible to touch the grinders when running and are essential where small children are around. As there is no need for a wall switch batch feed types are quicker and cheaper to install. They are also quieter than continuous feed models.

Waste disposers will deal with most food waste including: chicken carcasses, meat, fish eggshells, etc., but can jam on large bones and very hard fruit stones.

They must not be used for packaging materials such as: metal, plastic, rubber cloth, wool, glass, ceramics and string for which alternative bins will be needed.

There are different sizes available from $\frac{1}{2}$ to $\frac{3}{4}$ horsepower with guarantees from 2 to 10 years which is reflected in the price.

The most powerful models with the longest guarantees are the most expensive.

Size range from: 320–450 mm high × 150–230 mm diameter.

Some continuous feed models can be activated by *air switches* which can be fitted into the sink top or the surrounding worktop. They operate by pushing a button which sends a pulse of air to a microswitch which turns on the current at the socket positioned below the sink.

These can be used with wet hands with complete safety as there is no contact with the electric current.

Some models are fitted with an *automatic reversing switch* which prevents jamming and overheating.

Other cheaper models have a *reversing switch* which is useful if jams occur.

Air switch set into
sink surround

Air switch with under-sink
components for a waste
disposer – by In-Sink-Erator

Installation

Waste disposers should not discharge into cesspits nor into septic tanks of less than 2250 litres capacity.

They should never be run with hot water as this can cause grease to melt and line waste pipes.

Waste disposers need a 90 mm diameter sink waste outlet with a minimum 38 mm waste pipe connected to a P or S running trap (NOT a bottle trap) and be run with a minimum fall of 1:7 to ensure adequate flushing. The waste pipe should be taken directly to drain, with no other waste connections, in the shortest distance possible.

Some local authorities may ask for a 50-mm waste with an access gully or a stub waste and cleaning eye.

They use little electricity and require little maintenance but are noisy when running, increasingly so with age.

Refuse compactors

Domestic rubbish compactors are designed to compress all kitchen waste including empty cans, glass bottles and cartons. The compactor applies about $2\frac{1}{2}$ tons of force to compress everything down into a small tough plastic bag.

These packages take a very long time to decompose and could well become a problem for landfill sites.

Nowadays they are of doubtful domestic use as more and more local authorities are able to recycle separated waste.

They will fit under a standard worktop and are typically:

810 high $\times$ 510 deep $\times$ 310 wide mm.

Refuse Compactor with SS fascia and door front or can be supplied with fascia panel to match kitchen decor.
310 mm wide for building into standard kitchen cabinets by In-Sink-Erator

Sources: In-Sink-Erator, Tweeny

9
Cooking appliances

Cooking appliances can be broadly categorised as follows:

freestanding cooker
range cooker
built-in, split-level oven and hob
microwave oven

Freestanding cookers

Freestanding cookers combine an oven, grill and hob in one unit. They are generally cheaper and take up less room than either range cookers or built-in separate ovens and hobs.

Unfortunate visual result of fixing a freestanding cooker in with standard cabinets by breaking the plinth line

Their disadvantage is that, when slotted into a countertop, there are inevitable gaps on either side for dirt to accumulate and paper thin items to disappear.

They break up the run of cabinets visually as the worktop and plinth boards are not continuous.

A few freestanding cookers still have high level grills which are often popular but inhibit any storage above them for at least 300 mm and make a cooker hooded fan over the hob impracticable.

The oven is always at low level which is more difficult for easy access and visibility than an oven at waist level.

Most have depths of 600 mm to suit a standard worktop.

Common widths are 500, 600 and 630 mm.

Traditional range cookers

Range cookers with their cast iron construction and brightly coloured enamel doors have, for a long time, been a must-have item for the leisured classes in country houses. As they can cost as much as a new car and are expensive to run, they are inevitably a status symbol.

They are disliked by professional cooks for their lack of flexibility and unreliable oven and hob temperatures.

They are also not a good choice for busy working people – there is no thrusting two chops under a grill for a quick supper. If the insulated lids are left up for some time, the burners will cool down and take some time to regain heat.

Ideally they are 'on' all the time as cooling down causes condensation which results in rust.

However, despite all these disadvantages, they are loved by their owners for their comfortable room-warming properties and small details like the full length front rail for drying towels and overnight slow cooking in the bottom oven.

There are several different models: cooking only, cooking with a back boiler for hot water, cooking with a larger boiler for hot water and central heating for a limited number of radiators.

Typically there are two oven and four oven types, approximately 1 m and 1.5 m wide.

All models have at least a main oven and a second warming oven with two cast iron hot plates with insulated lids, one for boiling and one for simmering.

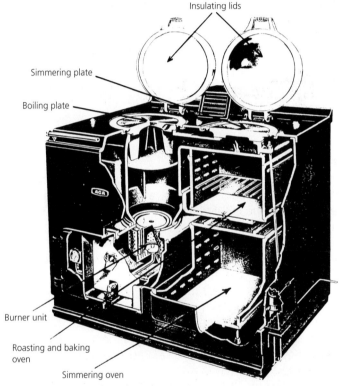

Insulating lids

Simmering plate

Boiling plate

Burner unit

Roasting and baking oven

Simmering oven

Two oven AGA cooker c. 1985

The depth is generally well over 600 mm so will protrude from a standard worktop and depending on type, some models require a 150 mm gap at one side for servicing and a 50 mm gap if positioned next to combustible materials such as a kitchen cabinet.

An electricity supply will be needed for those models with a pump and oven timer.

There are different models for the following fuels: natural or propane gas, electricity, kerosene, smokeless or bituminous coal, wood and peat briquettes.

They must sit on a concrete hearth of at least 125 mm thickness and all need an appropriate flue, except for electric models which need a vent to the outside air.

Source: Aga-Rayburn

New range cooker with gas hob, electric griddle and ovens with splashback and chimney cooker hood all in stainless steel – by Smeg

New range cookers

More recently, a modern version of the traditional range cooker has been developed which also has become a status symbol and a mark of the serious cook as they have 6–8 burners rather than 4 on a standard split-level hob and have either one very large oven or a medium oven with a smaller oven alongside. Some models also have warming and/or storage drawers.

They are generally 600 mm deep, so can align with standard worktops and come in 900, 1000, 1100 and 1200 mm widths.

Most are dual-fuel, gas hobs and electric ovens with integral grills. Some are all-electric or all-gas.

They look stylish generally finished in brushed stainless steel with cast iron griddles. Others are available in enamelled steel.

Apart from larger cooking areas, they do not perform any better than freestanding or split-level cookers.

Built-in ovens and hobs

Built-in, split-level ovens and hobs can be positioned in different parts of the kitchen or be fixed one above the other. Hobs can be inset anywhere in a worktop as their height is seldom more than 40 mm so do not interfere with drawers or cupboards underneath. Ovens can be positioned at waist level in tall cabinets or fitted under a countertop wherever required.

They are more expensive than freestanding cookers, not least because a cabinet housing will be needed for the oven.

There is also the opportunity to have different fuels for the two components. The perceived wisdom is that the best combination is a gas hob for instant and visible ease of adjusting the heat source and an electric oven which can be more precisely controlled and is slightly easier to keep clean.

Ovens – built-in

Individual ovens must have a grilling facility. Where there is only one oven, this will preclude roasting at the same time as grilling. Therefore two ovens are preferable – the second oven could in fact be a separate microwave oven with an integral grill. See p. 109.

The following features are desirable:

large glass viewing panel in the oven door
oven light
rotisserie – a revolving spindle for spit roasting
oven cleaning system (see below).

Ovens may have *side-hung* or *drop-down* doors.
Both have advantages. Side-hung doors do not get in the way and make for easier access. Drop-down doors provide a useful shelf for heavy vessels prior to moving them for serving.

Front panel finishes can be:
enamelled steel, stainless steel or aluminium.

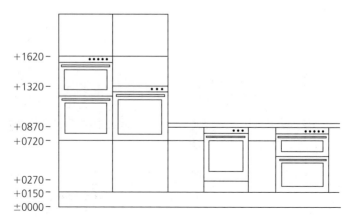

Typical heights of built-in single and double ovens

600 mm wide SS multifunction single oven – by Candy

600 mm wide polished SS multifunction double oven by Smeg

900 mm wide SS multifunction single oven with meat probe – by AEG

600 mm wide gas oven and grill – by New World

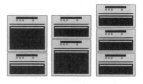

600 mm wide 'Compact' (i.e. low) single ovens available in various formats: self-cleaning multi-function oven, multi-function oven, steam oven, microwave oven which can be combined with one another or with standard size ovens according to choice – by Atag

Built-in electric and gas ovens

Microwave oven with trim for building into a 600 mm wide × 320 mm deep wall unit – by Neff

Freestanding combination microwave oven with grill by Baumatic

Steam oven for 600 mm wide unit by Miele

Steam oven shown with the water reservoir partly removed by Atag

Warming drawer (under oven) 140 mm high – by Gaggenau

Warming drawer 290 mm high – by Bosch

Built-in microwave, steam ovens and warming drawers

Electric oven types

Most electric ovens come with a variety of functions and are often described as 'multi-function'. The basic types are described below:

conventional	top and bottom elements for radiant heat cooking.
fan oven	fan at rear circulates, reducing the need for pre-heating, so saves time and can reduce cooking time.
grilling	radiant heat from top element, some ovens have a half grill option for smaller portions.
fan grilling	alternating between full grill and fan for a spit-roast effect.
bottom heat	bottom element only for a crisp underside for pizza and pastry bases.
defrosting	fan circulates air to speed up thawing.

These functions sometimes have proprietary names which can make comparing the merits of different ovens more difficult. There are also even more sophisticated variations of using these functions.

Steam ovens

The *steam oven* is the latest method of electric cooking.
The advantages of cooking with steam is that as the temperature never exceeds 100°C and as the food is not immersed in water, minerals and flavours are retained and protein can neither coagulate nor be lost through seepage, so that fish and meat stay tender and juicy. Also, nothing can burn or boil over so the oven is much easier to keep clean.

Steam cooking is also useful for bottling fruit, sterilising, melting chocolate and mulling wine.

In most types, no water supply is necessary as the steam comes from a reservoir which must be filled with (tap) water for every cooking session. The condensate is collected in a tray at the bottom which has to be emptied after cooking. More sophisticated models are available which can be connected to the water and drain pipes.

A limescale indicator will show when the descaling pro-gramme needs activating.

These ovens are equipped with racks and trays so that a variety of meat, fish and vegetables can be cooked simultaneously.

Note that steam comes out of the oven when the door is opened and therefore it is not considered safe to build them in under worktop level as they could scald children.

Warming drawers

Warming drawers are designed to pre-heat and keep food and plates warm in a drawer heated at 30–80°C.

The drawer(s) are usually stacked below the oven.

Gas ovens

Gas ovens are far simpler than electric ovens as the different heating zones are determined by the setting of the thermostat which corresponds to the central shelf while the top shelf is one gas mark above, the bottom shelf one gas mark below and the bottom of the oven still cooler.

Some cooks prefer to bake in a gas oven rather than an electric oven as the hot air is more moist.

The grill is incorporated in the top of a single oven or in a sep-arate smaller oven.

Built-in gas ovens are few and far between and tend only to be made by British manufacturers.

Oven cleaning systems

Pyrolytic cleaning works by heating the oven up to around 480°C for 1–3 hours which reduces food deposits to ash which can be swept away when the oven is cool.

Oxylytic linings are made up of microscopic porous oxygen-filled ceramic spheres. When the oven is heated up, oxygen is released causing food deposits to oxidise.

Catalytic liners are coated with a rough surfaced vitreous enamel that is activated by heating the oven to 220°C for half an hour which speeds up the process of burning off deposits.

Hydro-clean is a method of cleaning the oven by pouring 400 ml water and some detergent into the base of the oven and operating the bottom heating element to 60°C. This produces steam to loosen deposits which can be wiped out with a damp cloth when the oven is cool.

Enamel linings are sometimes provided at the bottom of the oven and also at the top of the oven which are removable for easier cleaning.

Microwave ovens

Microwave ovens, in one form or another are an essential appliance in today's kitchen. They may only be used for minor tasks such as defrosting, warming plates or reheating food or they may be the sole oven in the kitchen when conventional cooking is combined with microwaving as in the *combination microwave* which allows for extra speed and efficiency.

It is **the** essential appliance for busy young professionals working long hours who rely on ready-prepared frozen food for their evening meal.

How microwaves work

Microwaves are high frequency, short length, electromagnetic waves similar to TV radio waves. At the heart of the oven is a *magnetron* which converts the electric current into micro-frequency waves (2450 MHz for an 850 W oven).

Microwaves are reflected by metal, but can pass through most other materials.

They are particularly attracted to moisture. As microwaves enter the oven, they are scattered to distribute heat evenly either by *stirrers* or by a *turntable.* They reflect off the metal walls of the oven and pass through the non-metallic containers into the food. Here they cause molecules in the food to vibrate millions of times per second producing great heat which cooks the food.

Microwaves generate heat but are not hot in themselves.

Food will continue to cook after being removed from the oven, not by the microwaves but by the conduction of heat within the food. This is why some dishes need a certain amount of *standing time* before being served.

Safety

Microwaves, unlike X-rays and gamma rays, are *non-ionising* which means they do not build up in the body and do not change the structure of body cells. As a result they do not damage food chemically or build up radiation in the oven. Should microwaves leak from the oven, say from a faulty door seal, only a small amount would escape and this would decrease rapidly with distance from the oven.

Microwave ovens have to meet stringent emission criteria and the leakage level allowed is much lower than that which could cause harm. To prevent microwaves from escaping, doors are sealed electronically with at least two interlocking safety switches. This ensures the oven cannot be operated unless the door is completely closed and also that microwaves cease instantly the door is opened.

Pros and cons of microwave cooking

As microwaves cannot pass through the metal walls of the oven, they are remarkably energy efficient. Microwave ovens use only about 1 kW/h of energy as opposed to about 5 kW/h in many conventional ovens.

Microwaves do not shrink meat, destroy the taste or nutritional value of the food.

It is a valuable tool for quick thawing of frozen food, softening butter, melting chocolate, warming plates and heating hot drinks. However, some foods can become somewhat limp, when they should be crisp or brown. This can be remedied by choosing a microwave oven with a grill or multi-function oven.

Types of microwave oven

There are basically three types:

microwave cooking only	usually small and often freestanding
microwave with grill	good for browning meat, etc.
combination microwave	includes a grill and conventional oven elements and a fan.
	This provides six cooking methods:
	microwave only
	microwave plus grill
	microwave plus fan
	microwave plus grill and fan
	conventional oven
	grill only

Built-in models are designed to suit 500 and 600 mm wide cabinets.

Freestanding models can also sometimes be built-in with a proprietary kit.

There are a few small models with a depth of 300 mm designed to be fixed under standard wall cabinets.

Power rating

The power output of most microwave ovens can be: 600, 800, 900, 950 or 1000 watts.

The higher the power the faster the cooking.

Some foods, however, such as those with a great deal of water, fat or sugar may curdle if cooked too fast so lower power and a longer time is needed.

As a result there are different power levels which can range from 4 to 10. Normally 5 or 6 is used.

These numbers relate to different functions and starting with the lowest numbers, they are used for:

keeping food warm, defrosting, roasting, baking, cooking vegetables and heating liquids.

Typical sizes

small freestanding microwave oven:

17 litres = 460 w × 300 d × 460 h mm

large combination microwave oven:

30 litres = 595 w × 500 d × 460 h mm

Features

Some or all of the following features may be included:

automatic programmer	oven will select appropriate power level and cooking time suitable for type and weight of food
sensor cooking	measures moisture level or food temperature to detect when food is cooked
memory	allows for personal programmes to be stored

timer
pre-set/delayed start
normal or touch controls

Accessories

The following accessories may be included or optional extras:

removable metal rack	
removable glass shelf	
build-in kit	for fixing freestanding models into cabinets
temperature probe	plugs into internal socket and is inserted into food and desired temperature selected. When this is reached power is switched off. Useful for large joints and poultry

Maintenance

Metal objects other than the manufacturer's metal racks should never be used in microwave ovens. If metal comes into contact with the oven, sparks will fly which may cause damage.

It is important to keep door seals clean and replaced immediately if damaged.

Vents which let out steam should be kept clean.

It is particularly important for freestanding models with rear vents that they are not placed too close to a wall.

Repairs should only be undertaken by a qualified microwave service engineer.

Hobs – built-in

Natural or LPG (*liquid petroleum gas*) i.e. bottled gas is usually the preferred fuel for hob cooking as the heat can be adjusted visually very quickly by raising or lowering the flame.

Both gas and electric hobs are available in 2, 3, 4, 5 and 6 burner sizes – four burners being standard. Burners vary in size and are typically described as *rapid, medium rapid* and *simmering.*

Typical sizes (mm)	w	d	h
2 burner*	290	520	45
3 burner	520 diameter		45
4 burner	580	520	45
5 burner	700	520	45
6 burner	870	520	45

* Two burner units are often referred to as *domino* or *modular* hobs. These can be assembled in any combination of gas and electric models. See illustration on p. 116.

Gas hobs
Hob base plates are made in various materials: stainless steel, enamelled steel – usually white, black or brown and cast iron.

Ignition can be *push button* or *under knob* where gas lights automatically when a control knob is turned on.

Some models include a *flame failure* device which will turn off the gas supply if the flame is accidentally extinguished. A useful safety device if a hob is quite near an operable window or outside door.

A common accessory is a *wok stand* designed for a particular burner to support the bowl-shaped bottom of a traditional wok. Most models come with an *LPG conversion kit* for bottled gas.

900 mm wide 5 burner gas hob with central wok burner and cast iron supports – by AEG

700 mm wide 5 individual gas burners on glass hob with aluminium frame and cast iron pan stands – by Zanussi

520 mm round 3 gas burners on glass hob with cast iron pan stands by Baumatic

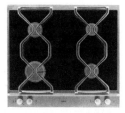

600 mm wide 4 gas burners on glass hob with cast iron pan supports – by AEG

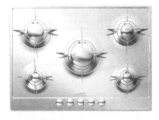

720 mm 5 burner gas hob in polished SS designed by Renzo Piano – by Smeg

600 mm SS 4 burner gas hob with enamelled pan supports by Zanussi

Gas hobs

Electric solid plate hobs

Solid plate hobs are the cheapest type of electric hob, but they are largely being superseded by *ceramic* and *induction* hobs (see below) which are more sophisticated and easier to keep clean.

The element is sealed within the plate so that the heat is distributed evenly and is thermostatically controlled. A useful safety feature is an on/off warning light.

Electric ceramic hobs

Ceramic hobs have halogen heating zones set under black ceramic tops. They may also include one or more *dual ring* zones which can extend the area, if required, to accommodate larger pans or fish kettles.

The zones are operated either by *control knobs* or *touch controls.*

Other features available:

fast cooking zone
automatic cut-out   – cuts off the power if electricity
sensor   – controls are damaged, or if a
                                 hob is left 'on' inadvertently
                                 it will switch off the power
                                 after a period of time.

residual heat indicator
cooking timer
emergency stop   – switches off all zones at once
child lock   – prevents children altering the
                                 controls.

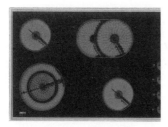

800 mm wide 6 zone ceramic hob
with control knobs and residual
heat indicators – by Zanussi

520 mm round frameless 3 zone
ceramic hob with touch controls
by Baumatic

914 mm wide 4 zone induction
hob in bevel edged glass
by Miele

320 mm wide hexagonal ceramic
hobs with one hexagon as control
panel which can be arranged in a
variety of honeycomb patterns
by Küppersbusch

600 mm wide 4 zone solid
plate hob – by Zanussi

Electric hobs

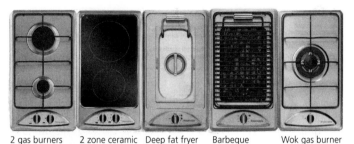

2 gas burners   2 zone ceramic   Deep fat fryer   Barbeque   Wok gas burner

SS Domino hobs – by Baumatic

Electric induction hobs

Induction hobs are the most expensive type of electric hob. They are more energy efficient that other types as about 75% of the energy is used to heat the pan compared with about 43% for a gas hob. The smaller the pan, the less energy is consumed.

Induction hobs heat the pan by magnetic heat transmission. The act of placing a pan on a heating zone causes the coil situated below the ceramic surface to generate heat almost instantaneously. Only the area under the pan is heated – the surrounding area stays cool. Heating stops once the pan is removed. As the temperature is lower than that of standard ceramic hobs, spillages do not burn so they are easier to keep clean and safer to use.

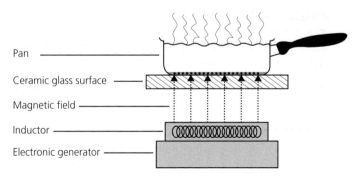

Pan

Ceramic glass surface

Magnetic field

Inductor

Electronic generator

Induction cooking

10
Extractors and cooker hoods

Building Regulations require that all domestic kitchens must be equipped with an extractor fan and providing the fan is of sufficient size, cooker hoods are accepted. See below.

A *cooker hood* is an extractor fan enclosed within a hood with a grease filter incorporated in the underside.

There are two sorts of cooker hood: those for *extracting air* to outside and those for *re-circulating* air over a carbon filter and back into the kitchen to remove the cooking smells.

Needless to say re-circulating models are a poor substitute for extractor hoods and are only of some slight use if it is utterly impracticable to install a duct to the outside.

The type and size of cooker hood will depend upon the lifestyle and the size of the kitchen. The near professional cook with a large kitchen and an adjacent dining area will need a powerful fan, while a small flat with a minute kitchen can make do with the smallest size that will satisfy the Building Regulations.

Extraction performance

Although the Building Regulations lay down a minimum extraction rate for a kitchen fan, this may well not be large enough to be effective. See pp. 72, 73.

The recommended air changes per hour for domestic kitchens is 10 to 15.

To calculate the size of fan required:

Find the volume of the room in cubic metres (m^3)
Multiply the volume of the room in cubic metres by the number of air changes per hour required

For example:

$$\text{kitchen} = 4\,\text{m} \times 5\,\text{m} \times 2.5\,\text{m} = 50\,\text{m}^3$$
$$\text{air changes required} = 12$$
$$50 \times 12 = 600\,\text{m}^3/\text{h}$$

Manufacturers' catalogues give the maximum and minimum extract rates in litres/second and cubic metres/hour.

one m^3/h = 0.777 l/s
one l/s = 3.6 m^3/h

Extractor fan outputs range from about 200 to 800 m^3/h

Depending on size, extractor fans in cooker hoods are approximately rated between 220 to 380 W.

Siting of fans

The most common cause of unsatisfactory mechanical ventilation is short circuiting of air movement between the fan and nearby air inlets, such as open windows or external doors.

Fans should be mounted as far as possible from such sources to work effectively.

Insufficient air replacement can also cause problems especially in well insulated houses with draught-proof windows.
If necessary make provision for air replacement with gaps under room doors, internal grilles in doors, airbricks, etc.

Fans and cooker hoods should not be positioned above a high level grill, nor should the underside of a cooker hood be too low over a hob for fear of catching fire.
Each fan manufacturer will give recommended clearances.
Typically they may be:

65 mm minimum over a gas hob
55 mm minimum over an electric hob.

Ducting

Ducts from extractor fans should ideally be as short as possible and as close to an outside vent grille as possible.
For maximum efficiency a duct should be no longer than 5 m deducting 1.2 m for every 90° bend.

Ducts should rise up immediately a minimum of 300 mm from the extractor fan before any bends to avoid turbulence.

Where possible use 45° bends rather than 90° bends.
If 90° bends are necessary, use large radius bends.

Suitable materials for extractor fan ducts are:

   rigid PVC, galvanised sheet steel and flexible aluminium

Avoid *spiral-concertina* hoses which reduce air flow and generate noise by flapping.

Avoid any *flat* ducting (rectangular in section) as these will considerably reduce performance.

Horizontal ducts should have a 25 mm fall to outside to get rid of any condensate.

Long vertical ducts may need *condensation traps* to allow condensate to evaporate.

Duct diameters should always be the same size as the outlet from the extractor and never reduced.
Usual sizes are: 100, 120 and 150 mm diameter

Terminate ducts on the outside wall with a louvered grille incorporating a *back-draught shutter.*

Noise

Extractor fans are noisy – the larger amount of air extracted the greater the noise.

Check when a powerful fan is required that the noise levels are tolerable.

The decibel rating for different sizes of fans ranges from 50 to 70 dB(A) re 1 pW.

Types of cooker hood

There are six basic different types of cooker hood:

Chimney	large wall-mounted hood, sometimes made to suit range cookers with big skirt and chimney in matching material
Island	similar to chimney hood but for a hob in an island situation
Integrated	concealed in wall cabinet with top hung pull-out flap matching cabinet doors.
Telescopic	slimline hood with motor concealed in wall cabinet operated by full-width narrow pull-out section at base
Canopy	concealed behind a fixed panel matching cabinet doors with air intake grille set level with bottom of panel
Standard	wall-mounted over hob with extract duct behind wall cabinet door

All cooker hoods incorporate grease filters. The best are made of stainless steel which can be washed in a dishwasher.

Cheaper models have disposable paper filters which typically need changing twice a year.

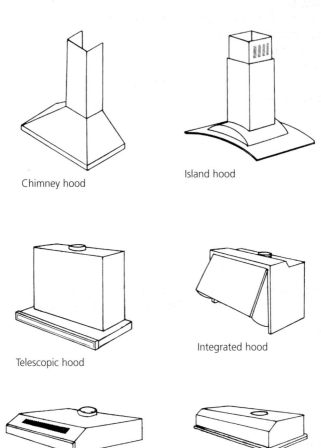

Chimney hood

Island hood

Telescopic hood

Integrated hood

Standard hood

Canopy hood

Basic types of cooker hood

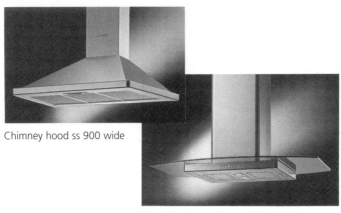

Chimney hood ss 900 wide

Island hood ss and glass 900 wide

Canopy hood 524 wide

Integrated hood 600 wide

Telescopic hood 600 wide

Cooker hoods – by Baumatic

Standard hood 600 wide

Cooker hood features

The following features may be included:

lights	typically 2 × 20 W halogen lamps
speed level switch	usually for 3 levels
automatic sensor	humidistat
run-on facility	timer set for fan to overrun
interval ventilation	to ventilate room periodically
charcoal filter	for re-circulating models
grease filter	for extraction models
saturation indicator	for filter changing/washing
splashback	matching splashback, often sold together with range cookers

Hob extractors

In addition to the extractors described above, there are also *hob extractors*. These are NOT suitable for gas hobs and are not as efficient as overhead cooker hoods. However, they can be useful alongside electric barbeque hobs which can emit noxious fumes at hob level or where uninterrupted headroom or view is desirable.

They are designed to be set alongside domino hobs in island or peninsular worktops. They extract the air downwards through 125 mm diameter ducts into base cabinets and horizontally to outside.

The fan is positioned either at the bottom of the base cabinet or externally at the end of the horizontal duct.

It is not always easy to accommodate the horizontal duct unless there is convenient floor joist space or it can be carried along the ceiling of a floor below.

See illustration overleaf.

Hob extractor with automatic sealing flaps – shown open-operated by touch control panel

Hob extractor with grille alongside electric hobs operated by control knob

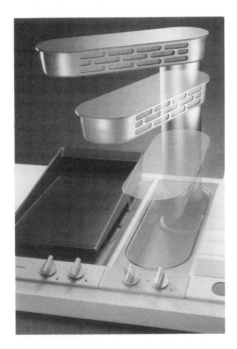

Installation drawing of direct suction hob extractor with duct in base cabinet turning horizontally to link with remote fan on outside wall

Direct suction hob extractor with 90° rotating arm which can extend to 420 mm above hob. Contracts back flush with worktop when not in use.

Hob extractors – by Gaggenau

11
Cooling appliances

The choice of cooling appliances depends upon the shopping habits of the clients and the space available in the kitchen.

As the third component of the *kitchen triangle*, the refrigerator is both an essential and frequently used appliance.

Urban dwellers with no children and no garden, with easy access to local shops and who do not mind frequent shopping trips, can make do with a relatively small refrigerator compared with the large family in a country house.

In the very large household, a north facing larder or a cold room will reduce the need for a large refrigerator and with a freezer in an outhouse, a fridge-freezer would be all that is needed in the actual kitchen.

Model types

The various types and combinations of refrigerators and freezers can be loosely categorised as:

refrigerator with icebox	with small freezing compartment
larder refrigerator	with no freezing compartment
fridge-freezer	refrigerator stacked with freezer
'side-by-side'	American style, wide fridge-freezer with two doors, often with ice and chilled water dispenser
'bottom freezer'	fridge-freezer with bottom drawer as freezer
wine store	refrigerator set at 10°C for wine, cigars and cheese
upright freezer	freezer with side hung door
chest freezer	freezer with hinged lid

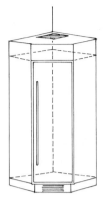

Corner refrigerator
1650 × 1050 mm
on plan

Typical integrated in-
column refrigerator
stacked on top of freezer

Typical large chest freezer
500 litres with counter-
balanced lid

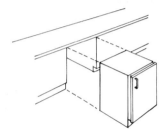

Typical integrated built-under
refrigerator or freezer

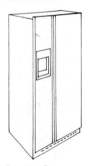

Freestanding
American style
Side-by-side refri-
gerator typically:
900 w × 660 d ×
1800 h

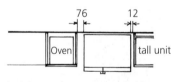

Typical minimum clearances needed for
side-by-side freestanding refrigerator
between oven and tall unit

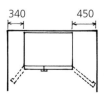

Typical minimum
clearance needed to
remove drawers from
interior of freestand-
ing side-by-side
refrigerator

Fully integrated fridge-
freezer with ice dispenser
by Gaggenau

Freestanding
corner refriger-
ator in SS
by Norcool

Freestanding 'Bottom
Freezer' with freezing
compartment in bottom
drawer – by Gaggenau

Temperature control cabinet
with three climate zones for
red wine, white wine, cheese
and cigars – by Gaggenau

Refrigeration
unit for cold
room or
wine cellar
by Norcool

So-called '50's
style refriger-
ator available
in silver and
seven colours
by Smeg

Fitting format

Most of the different models listed above are available as:

freestanding	usually cheap small models or large side-by-side and 'retro style' (i.e. with rounded corners) fridge-freezers
built-in	generally means appliance will fit into 500 or 600 mm wide spaces to suit standard cabinets with facility for a 'decor' panel to match cabinet door fronts
in-column	means appliances built into tall cabinets, sometimes stacked one above the other. This may mean they are fully integrated but also, confusingly, can mean 'built-in' Check with the manufacturer
built-under	as 'built-in' (above) but low enough to fit under a standard 900 mm high worktop so is about 865 mm high
fully integrated	can be built into standard tall or base cabinets, accept matching doors and variable plinth heights

Note that *fully integrated* appliances fit seamlessly into standard cabinets.

Built-in and *built-under* appliances, which are not fully integrated, will have dirt trapping gaps at the sides and will break the continuous plinth line of adjacent cabinets.

Cooling appliances unless *freestanding* will need ventilation space at the back and at plinth level to suit manufacturer's requirements.

Side-by-side fridge-freezers are generally larger than a 600 mm deep worktop. They take up a lot of floor space and need from 250 to 450 mm both sides for full access to door storage. See p. 126.

Those with ice and water dispensers need a water connection.

Capacity

The volume of different models can vary from as little as 120 litres for a built-under larder refrigerator to 600 litres for a side-by-side fridge-freezer.

As a guide, allow about 28 litres (one cubic foot) for each person in the household.
This volume may be reduced if there is a separate freezer.

Most families find that 140–170 litres is adequate.

For the household with a kitchen garden, a total of 400 litres may be more suitable. Here a 250 litre chest freezer outside the kitchen and a refrigerator in the kitchen might be appropriate.

Defrosting

There are three methods:

manual   appliance is turned off, contents removed and ice left to thaw and drain from the bottom shelf into a bowl

auto defrost during normal operation, ice builds up on the back wall which subsequently melts and runs down the back wall into a container from which it is evaporated by the heat of the compressor.

frost free   sensors monitor the temperature and direct a fan at the back of the appliance to circulate chilled air through a system of vents evenly round the interior. This has the benefit that frozen packs do not stick together, labels stay legible and ice never builds up. However, it can make food somewhat dry, is expensive to run and tends to be less energy efficient.

Controls

The adjustable thermostats and the on/off switches should be easily visible and accessible.

Note that the numbers on the thermostats do not refer to temperatures. Normally (but not always), the higher the number, the colder the temperature.

Warning lights in freezers should be seen at a glance.

With fridge-freezers, it is much more convenient, but more expensive to have separate controls for the two compartments, particularly if the freezer has to be defrosted manually, this allows the refrigerator still to operate.

Refrigerator features

Some or all of the following features may be included:

adjustable shelves	wire/glass/plastic
interior light	
rollers	useful for servicing
ice cube tray	
egg tray	usually in door
dairy compartment	usually in door
wine rack	usually in door
wine/cheese compartment	set at 10°C
salad drawer (crisper)	usually at bottom

Freezer features

Some or all of the following features may be found in freezers:

food drawers	wire/clear or solid plastic
interior light	
warning light	
acoustic alarm	useful for freezer in outhouse
thermometer	

fast-freeze switch
handle lock
ice and chilled water dispenser

or fast-freeze compartment
useful for freezer in outhouse

Temperature zones

Some refrigerators have compartments with different temperature zones. Typically this may be a relatively warm +10°C
drawer for wine, cheese, etc.

Some have a salad/crisper drawer where the humidity can be
adjusted for optimum freshness of fruit and vegetables. This
drawer is the warmest part of the fridge and is generally found
at the bottom where it picks up heat from the compressor.

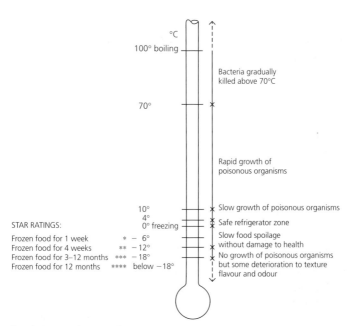

Food storage temperatures

The coldest part of the fridge, between 0 and 5°C, is usually the lower two shelves, but refrigerators with an ice box at the top have the coldest part immediately under the ice box.

Upper shelves and door storage will be cool zones +5° to 7°C suitable for dairy and wine storage.

In frost-free appliances, the temperature is even throughout the interior.

Star ratings

Star ratings for freezers and ice boxes are as follows:

*	= −6°C	suitable for storing pre-frozen food for a week
**	= −12°C	suitable for storing pre-frozen food for 4 weeks
***	= −18°C	suitable for storing pre-frozen food for 3 to 12 months
****	= −18°C (or colder)	suitable for storing frozen food for 12 months and freezing fresh food up to 1/10th volume of freezer without using a fast-freeze facility.

Climate class

All cooling appliances are ascribed a climate class. This denotes the range of *room temperatures* that an appliance is designed to operate within effectively:

N	= +16°–32°C
SN	= +10°–32°C
N-ST	= +16°–38°C
SN-ST	= +10°–38°C

Noise levels

Some appliances can be a great deal noisier than others. Models which work by absorption are quieter but more expensive than those with compressors.

Noise levels are given for all cooling appliances and are expressed in decibels as dB(A) re 1 pW.
These range from low at about 33 to high at 47 decibels.

Energy consumption

All cooling appliances are given an energy-efficient class. These rate from A (good) to G (bad).
Most fridges and freezers are rated A or B.

Frost-free refrigeration tends to be less energy efficient.

All appliances should carry the *EU energy label* which describes the manufacturer, model number, energy efficiency class, energy consumption (kW/cycle), net volume of fresh and frozen food compartments (litres), noise levels (dB(A) re 1 pW). See pp. 40, 41.

Running costs can be high as cooling appliances operate all hours every day.
Most manufacturers state energy consumption for 24 hours (kWh) and an indication of annual running costs (£/kWh).

Larders and cold rooms

Before refrigeration was invented, houses were equipped with *larders*, either in an outhouse or in a north-facing room where part of the window would be fitted with perforated or woven copper or brass screens to let in the cool air but keep the insects out. The room would be lined with slate shelves and the ceiling fitted with hooks on which to hang game.

This type of room can of course be replicated as it is particularly useful for keeping cheese, fresh fruit and vegetables, prepared and left-over food.

Today it is possible to create a cold room without the need for north-facing outside walls by using two basic components – a *refrigeration unit* and a *cold room door*. The walls (and floor if necessary) should be suitably insulated.

Refrigeration units are designed for temperatures of 3–12°C and for different sized rooms. They are also available as 'split units' where the warm and cold parts are separately installed – the cold part inside the room and the warm part up to 12 m away in another room where heat emission is not a problem. The two components are connected by a copper pipe and electric wiring.

The cold room doors can be supplied with panelling to match the house doors or be faced in stainless steel. The door is insulated, has magnetic door seals and the inside is lined with storage boxes.

This type of installation is also suitable for making a *wine cellar*.

Source: Norcool

Green issues

Today the refrigerant and insulation of cooling appliances are CFC (chlorofluorocarbon) free and most are HFC (hydro fluorocarbon) free. However HFC, which does not deplete ozone, is still a powerful greenhouse gas.

The alternatives, which are more generally used today, are natural gases such as propane and isobutane which have no effect on global warming. Some appliances use a refrigerant called R600a which is considered safe.

Source: *Which?*

12
Dishwashers

Dishwashers, like many other appliances, are available as *free-standing, built-in* or *fully integrated* models.
See p. 128 for implications of these descriptions.

Full size models 600 mm wide × 850 mm deep claim to be large enough for 12 place settings.
Slim models 450 mm wide are available for 9 place settings.
There is also a *Compact* model 600 mm wide × 450 mm high for 6 place settings, for building into tall units.
All these models have a drop-down counterbalanced door.
There are also under worktop models with one or two *pull-out drawers* for 6 or 12 place settings.

Place setting

A place setting consists of:

240 mm diameter dinner plate
230 mm diameter soup plate
165 mm diameter side plate
140 mm diameter saucer
 87 mm diameter cup

120 mm high glass
knife and fork
soup spoon
dessert spoon
teaspoon

Drying

In most machines, dishes are dried from the heating element at the base of the machine.
Some model have *active drying* where the steam is carried away by convection.
More expensive models have a *fan* which circulates the hot air to speed up the drying time.

Energy

Dishwashers should display an energy label which will give ratings from A (good) to G (bad) for:
energy efficiency (A–G), energy consumption (kWh/cycle), cleaning performance (A–G), drying performance (A–G), number of place settings, water consumption (litres/cycle) and noise (dB(A) re 1 pW). See p. 40.

Manufacturers sometimes advertise their models as:

   A,A,B (energy/washing/drying) or B,B,C

They claim that dishwashers are more energy efficient than hand washing as they use little more than two sink bowls of water, 14 to 16 litres of water being typical figures for dishwasher consumption.

Half load programmes may save only 10–20% of water so they are not as efficient as waiting until the dishwasher is full. Reducing the amount of water rather than the temperature makes for a more efficient wash.

Water connection

Most manufacturers recommend cold fill only. Previously, if there was hot water in the house heated by gas or oil, it was more efficient to connect to this supply. Today, however, machines are much more sophisticated and have programmes with water temperatures ranging from cold to 70°C (see p. 139) so the machine would not be able to adjust the temperature of the centrally heated water down from say 60°C to 50°C for an economy wash.

Another factor is that water should not be too hot when first entering the machine as food residues will tend to stick to the crockery rather than be washed off.

Noise

Dishwashers are noisy.
Better models have good sound absorbing linings to the casing.
Decibel ratings range from about 43 to 59 dB(A).

Features

The following features may be included:

hinged cup rack in upper basket	
height adjustable upper basket	useful if large diameter plates need to fit in rack underneath
foldable rack in bottom basket	provides more room for pans
refill warning lights	for rinse-aid and salt replacement
time delay switch	useful for economy tariff when machines can be run at night
child safety lock	prevents door being opened during cycle
anti-flooding device	detects leaks in hose and shuts off water supply

450 mm wide freestanding dishwasher for 9 place settings in SS – by Smeg

600 mm wide semi-integrated dishwasher with SS door for 12 place settings – by Candy

600 mm wide double 'Dish Drawer' in embossed SS for 6 + 6 place settings by Fisher & Paykel

600 w × 480 d × 460 h fully integrated 'compact' dishwasher for 6 place settings – by AEG

Dot matrix function display control panel on top edge of fully integrated dishwasher door – by Küppersbuch

Dishwashers

Programmes

Typical programmes to be found are:

pre-wash	cold water rinse when machine not used daily
half load wash	uses 10–12% less water
quick wash	30°C for 30 min
delicate wash	40°C for fine glass and china
economy wash	50°C (may not remove tea stains)
normal wash	65°C
intensive wash	65°C or 70°C with pre-wash
automatic	55–65°C, claims to select appropriate programme for maximum efficiency of water, energy and time

Programme times for a full size normal wash can vary from 120 to 155 min.

13
Storage

Storage of food, crockery, cutlery and utensils is at a premium in the kitchen. Few people think they have enough. However, having a large number of cupboards does not necessarily lead to an efficiently run kitchen.

Quite a number of items can be classified as occasional use only which may often be stored elsewhere, such as:
party crockery, vases, large cooking vessels such as preserving pan, fish kettle, ice bucket, jam jars and household cleaning materials.

Day to day essentials include:
saucepans, frying pan, colander, sieves, kitchen knives, wooden spoons, everyday china and cutlery, some dry goods and condiments.

It is generally considered necessary to have a minimum of $5\frac{1}{2}\,m^2$ of storage shelf area, excluding the refrigerator and cleaning materials.
Large households may need up to twice this amount.

Below is a list which relates basic items to the areas in which they belong. Items may be stored in cabinets, on open shelves or hung on hooks.

sink area:	detergents, scouring liquids, bleach, cloths, sponges, brushes, bucket, waste bins, washing-up bowl, colander, sieves
wet preparation area near sink:	chopping board, kitchen knives, scissors, string, foil, plastic bags, bin liners, drying-up cloths
dry preparation area:	dry goods, scales, mixing bowls, blender, electric whisk/food processor, rolling pin, pastry cutters, baking tins, cook books

hob:	saucepans, frying pan, casserole, grill pan, fish slice, serving spoon, ladle, wooden spoons, seasonings
refrigerator: 2–6°C	dairy produce, uncooked meat, salad, delicatessen, white wine, beer
larder: (if available, otherwise refrigerator) 6–12°C	fruit, vegetables, cheese, fats, eggs, cooked meat
freezer: −18°C or below	all food suitable for freezing which excludes: milk, mayonnaise (which may separate), hard boiled eggs, jellies, high water content vegetables
serving area:	china, glass, cutlery, table linen, condiments, trays

Wall storage

Where possible, hang as many things on the wall between the worktop and wall cupboards. These should be frequently used items as they will collect dust and grease if near the hob.

This area is ideal for: knife racks near the sink, utensil racks near the hob, spice jar racks, paper and cling film dispensers, wall-hung scales, can openers, wall telephone, etc.

Ceilings

Where a hob is placed in an island worktop, pots and pans may be suspended from the ceiling on racks.

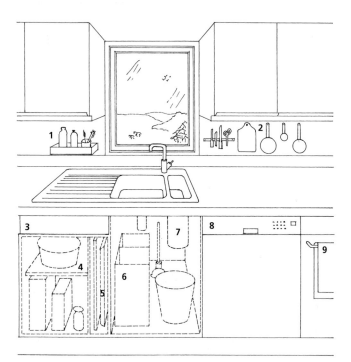

1 Washing-up utensils
2 Knife rack, chopping board, sieves
3 Drawer for food bags, bin bags, labels, ties, string, etc
4 Washing-up bowls, cleaning materials
5 Tray slot
6 Waste bins, bucket, plunger, etc
7 Waste disposer
8 Dishwasher
9 Towel hang on long 'D' handle

Storage – sink and wet preparation

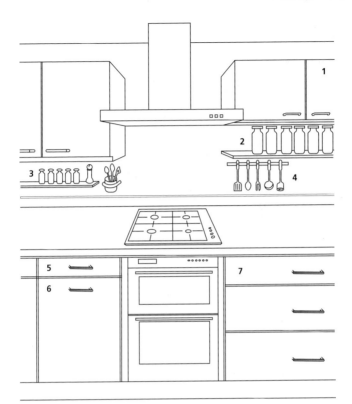

1 Flour, rice, pasta
2 Storage jars
3 Condiments, spices, herbs
4 Rack for large cooking utensils
5 Drawer for small cooking utensils
6 Pull-out drawer for wire baskets for baking tins
7 Pan drawers

Storage – cooking

14
Cabinets

Proprietary kitchen cabinets abound in many guises to suit different tastes and budgets.
The advantage for the client is that they can see the product either illustrated in glossy catalogues or displayed in showrooms. Another advantage of using proprietary cabinets is that although the ordering time may be lengthy, the fitting on site can be done reasonably quickly providing the demolition of any previous fittings has been undertaken along with the preparation of water, waste, heating and electrical services.

However, the cost of most ready-made fitted kitchens is generally exorbitant and often a 'rip-off'.
What the client pays for is the door and drawer fronts which, at the cheapest, will be melamine faced chipboard (MFC) and at the most expensive will be solid oak panels/stainless steel/solid gloss acrylic/satin aluminium roller shutters.

Most often, carcasses are made of standard 15 or 18 mm MFC. These can be bought separately and bespoke door and drawer fronts fitted separately.
Door fronts can be as cheap as 18 mm MDF hung and painted by the contractor on site.

Cabinets made of steel are also available and are particularly suitable where good hygiene is essential as they are impervious to water and insect damage. They are also fire resistant and can be a durable choice for domestic kitchens.
They are made of stainless steel or zinc coated steel finished in various polyester powder colours.

Kitchen manufacturers will often include a design service within their price, but where an architect is employed, this service will be redundant which results in the client paying more than is necessary.

Where the client desires purpose-made specially designed cabinets, the cost will inevitably be considerably higher than factory made units.

Cabinet sizes

The *British Standard range of kitchen cabinets* is based upon multiples of 100 mm.

Most proprietary European manufacturers conform to these dimensions, given here in millimetres:

Lengths of units:

base units	300, 400, 500, 600, 1000 and 1200
sink units	1000, 1200, 1500 and 1800
wall units	300, 400, 500, 600, 1000 and 1200
tall units	500 and 600

Heights* above finished floor level:

top of highest unit	1950–2250
highest shelf for general use	1800
underside of wall unit	1350
top of worktop	850, 870 and 920
underside of worktop	820, 870 and 920
top of plinth	100 (80 min)

* In practice the height dimensions are more typically as shown in section on p. 147.

Depths (front to back):

worktops	600
base units	600
sink units	600
tall units	600
wall units	300
toe recess	50 min (from front edge of worktop)

WALL UNITS

Open shelves   Open shelves   Single door   Double door   Glass door   Roller
at end   shutter

Two door   Diagonal   Corner
corner   corner

BASE UNITS

Single door   Double door   Single door   Double door   Housing   Tray/towel
                              under-sink   under-sink   for oven   slot

Single door   Double doors   Pull-out   Three drawers   Four drawers   Four wide
and drawer   and drawers   door   drawers

1/2 circle   3/4 circle   Full circle   Diagonal
carousel   carousel   carousel   corner
in corner   in corner   in diagonal
                              corner

TALL UNITS

5 shelves   Broom   Pull-out   Housing for   Housing for   Housing
             cupboard   larder   oven/fridge   ovens/fridge   for tall fridge

TYPICAL WIDTHS

Wall units : 300, 400, 500, 600, 800, 1000, diagonal corner 600 × 600
Base units : 300, 400, 500, 600, 800, 1000, diagonal corner 900 × 900
Tall units : 300 pull-out larder, 500, 600

LESS COMMON WIDTHS

Wall units : 450, 700, 900, 1100, 1200
Base units : 150 (open), 450, 900, 1100, 1200
Tall units : 400, 450

Kitchen cabinets – summary of basic types

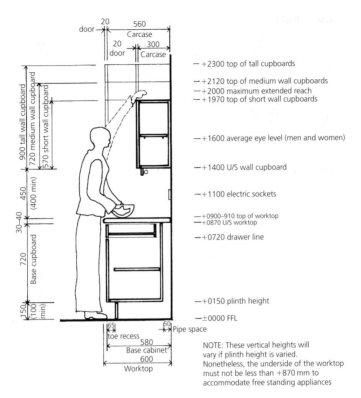

Typical cabinet detail dimensions

Setting-out dimensions

When planning a kitchen layout, allow for tolerance in dimensions. Even in new buildings, corners may not be absolutely square nor plaster finishes completely flat.

When laying out a kitchen within existing buildings and where the dimensions are not convenient for standard units, leftover space may usefully accommodate a tray slot or a pull-out towel rail. This will be cheaper than specifying a cabinet of a non-standard width.

Dimensions to watch on plan

When using a 1000 mm wide corner base unit, a *corner post* is generally needed. This post is usually L-shaped, 60 × 60 mm. Check with the manufacturer whether any extra millimetres need to be added to the worktop length to accommodate the post. See illustration on p. 36.

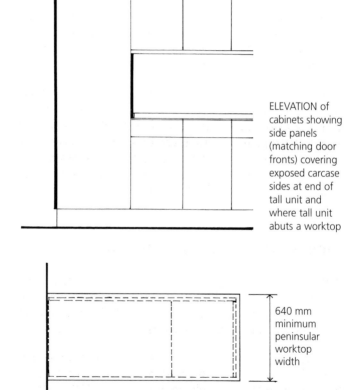

ELEVATION of cabinets showing side panels (matching door fronts) covering exposed carcase sides at end of tall unit and where tall unit abuts a worktop

640 mm minimum peninsular worktop width

PLAN of peninsular worktop showing side panels (matching door fronts) covering exposed carcase sides at end and back

Where drawers are at right angles to one another in a corner, check that when one drawer is opened it does not foul on the handle of the other. This can happen where long linear handles, such as D handles are used.

Standard 600 mm deep worktops project 40 mm in front of most carcases. This means the worktop will project from 19 to 25 mm in front of the cabinet doors depending on the thickness of the doors which can vary from 15 mm for cheap MFC to 21 mm, say, for solid oak panelled doors.

Where a single bank of cabinets is placed under a *peninsular worktop*, a back panel and a side panel to match the doors will be needed. This means the depth of the peninsular worktop must be at least a non-standard depth of 640 mm.

Where a base unit abuts a tall unit, the *carcase side* of the tall unit will be exposed above the worktop. If the sight of white melamine faced chipboard is not desirable then a full length panel matching the door fronts can be inserted. Similarly, a tall cupboard at the end of a run may need a full length panel to cover the exposed side of the carcase. This will add an extra 15–21 mm on plan, depending on door thickness.

Dimensions to watch on section

Worktops are generally 30–40 mm thick. This dimension of 10 mm will not affect the overall height of the cabinets but will affect the distance between the top of the worktop and the underside of any wall cupboards.

Cabinets are supported on *adjustable legs* behind a plinth board. These will affect the overall height of the cabinets.
They are normally available in three sizes: 100, 120 and 150 mm.
This latitude allows the height of the worktop to be adjusted to suit the client.

Carcase construction

Carcases are made from 15 or 18 mm thick melamine faced chipboard (MFC) with all exposed edges lipped with melamine tape. Cheaper ranges will be made from 15 mm MFC and may have hardboard rather than MFC backs.
Carcases can be supplied *rigid* or *packed flat*, the latter being cheaper to buy, but may cost more for the contractor to assemble.

Base units have MFC or hardboard backs set in 50 mm to allow for pipe runs.

Drawers, which may be plastic, wooden or have metal sides are generally supplied fully assembled together with metal runners.

Shelves are usually supported on adjustable socket and peg shelf supports. Tall 'larder' cupboards may have one fixed centre shelf for rigidity.

Doors, if supplied, will normally be fitted with 90° concealed hinges which can be adjusted to align the doors correctly.

Plinth boards can be attached to plates with clips which clip on to the adjustable legs supporting the cabinets.

Free-standing cabinets

Free-standing, ready-made kitchen cabinets can be bought from shops and furniture warehouses. These have the benefits of fast delivery and being transportable, should the clients wish to take them on to their next home.
Otherwise the disadvantages are lack of flexible planning and impractical and unhygienic gaps between units.

There is, of course, the vogue for having a kitchen with completely free-standing cupboards and appliances, harking back to large nineteenth century kitchens with a cooking range, a big dresser and a large central wooden table. This is coupled with the idea of not wanting the kitchen to look too 'stream-lined' or 'minimalist'.

However, for sheer efficiency and for cooking in a hygienic environment, there is nothing to beat the continuous worktop with appliances built into cabinets above a continuous plinth. Also, the exposed legs of free-standing units make the area underneath inaccessible and difficult to clean, which all too soon becomes colonised by undesirable creatures.

Cabinet accessories

Whether cabinets are bought off-the-peg or purpose-built or assembled from standard carcases with purpose-made doors, some of the accessories which go inside the cabinets are certainly worth considering. These can be bought from specialist kitchen hardware suppliers. The number of items is endless but they can be summarised as:

Support fittings

Adjustable feet, long legs for table/peninsular worktops, cabinet and worktop support brackets, internal shelf supports, wall cabinet hangers, worktop connection fittings, brackets for small microwave oven and TV.

Hardware

Hinges, door flap and lift-up fittings, door and drawer handles, knobs and continuous pulls, catches, stays, worktop edging, cornice profiles.

Drawers

Moulded plastic drawers, wooden drawers, metal drawer sides, runners, dividers, insert trays.

Shelves and baskets

Wirework baskets, wicker baskets, shelves, pull-out larder shelving, pull-out column shelving, wine racks, carousel shelves for corner cupboards.

Rails

Midway rail systems for hanging various attachments, such as utensil rack, spice rack, knife block, roll holder, book rest.

Waste bins

Door-hung bins, bins in various combinations sliding out on runners, foot-operated door opener for bin cabinet.

Miscellaneous

Telescopic towel rail, folding steps, first aid cabinet, radio designed to fit under standard wall cabinet.

Sources: Blum, Häfele, Isaac Lord, Woodfit

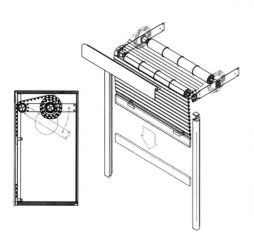

ROLLER SHUTTER
CABINET DOOR
'Tambour' system in
aluminium coated
plastic suitable for
500 and 600 mm
wide cabinets 720 or
1210 mm high

LIFT-UP SPRING
HINGE for
flaps of top
boxes of cabi-
net tall units

   120°

CONCEALED HINGE for
standard cabinet lay-on
doors. 120° opening angle
with spring closing mechanism. Similar hinges for
100°, 107° and 170°
opening

ADJUSTABLE PLINTH FOOT
with clip and bracket for
fixing to plinth board

Cabinet door and support fittings

'MAGIC' CORNER UNIT optimises space in 1000 mm corner base units.
Door pulls out first set of trays and then swings sideways which moves the second set of trays out from blind corner

PULL-OUT BASKETS. Chrome plated wire baskets for 400–1000 mm wide base units

PULL-OUT LARDER. Centre-mounted, height adjustable wire baskets for 300, 500 and 600 mm wide tall units

CAROUSEL TRAYS. $\frac{1}{2}$ round chrome wire trays for 900 and 1000 mm wide corner base units

CAROUSEL TRAYS. $\frac{3}{4}$ circle chrome wire trays for 900 × 900 mm corner base unit

Wire shelving for cabinet interiors

FIRST AID
CABINET
lockable
260 × 182 ×
245 w

GLASS RACK for fitting inside
500 mm wide tall or wall units

STEP STOOL for
storing in plinth
space 390 w ×
390 d × 385 h
unfolded
390 w ×
95 d × 465 w
folded

WINE RACK for
300 mm wide
base unit

MICROWAVE
WALL BRACKETS
adjustable
330–460 mm

SLIDING TOWEL RAIL in
chrome for side or top fixing
under worktop - L or R hand
480 l (closed) × 102 w × 36 w

ROLL HOLDER for
cling film foil and
paper towels 352 w ×
150 d × 305 w

SPICE RACK for
door interiors
395 w × 55 d ×
500 h

CUTLERY INSERT two
tier in white plastic for
500 mm wide drawer

Cabinet and wall-hung fittings

15
Worktops

The worktop is the most important visual element in the kitchen. This large horizontal area is the first to meet the eye. It is also the place where all the preparation and serving of cooking takes place.

Worktops for kitchens should be hardwearing, heatproof, water resistant, not too hard to break crockery, but not too soft to be easily scored with a knife, light in colour – both to reflect light and to disguise food residues which tend to be light in colour (dark colours also show up scratches, dust and wear), and last but not least, good to look at.

A tough specification and some compromises will be inevitable when selecting a finish for a top.
Sheet materials are essential. Joints in tiles or mosaics are soft and quickly ingrained with dirt, so become a breeding ground for undesirable bacteria as well as looking unattractive.

There are no perfect surfaces, most will be marred by very hot pans, so trivets should always be to hand or stainless steel pan supports inserted near the hob.
All will be spoilt by heavy scoring, so chopping boards should always be used.

Fabricating worktops is a specialised and often expensive business. Where possible employ specialist contractors to measure and make templates on site, prefabricate, deliver, fix and finally clean/seal/polish on site.

Plastic laminate faced worktops

Plastic laminate is still one of the most practical and cheapest materials for facing kitchen worktops.

It is made up of several sheets of *kraft* (Swedish for strong) *paper* and a printed decorative sheet protected with a transparent melamine overlay. These are impregnated with thermosetting resins and fused together under heat and high pressure. Typical sheet size: 3660 × 1525 × 0.8 mm with some patterns available up to 4100 mm long.

The laminate is abrasion, scratch and impact resistant, also heat resistant up to 180°C for short periods. It is hygienic and can be kept clean with water and mild detergents and non-scratch liquids so it is an ideal, maintenance-free, decorative surface for domestic kitchen worktops.

Grades and finishes

Plastic laminates are available in several grades such as: general purpose, post forming and vertical surfaces.

These sheets are also available in various finishes most typically *velour* (satin), gloss and matt.

Surface textures can also vary between flat, granular and heavily textured.

The most suitable choice for kitchen worktops are light colours with small patterns. These show least scratches and abrasions. Avoid dark, heavily textured or gloss finished laminates.

Wood laminates

There are two types of wood laminates – those using real wood veneers and cheaper versions using photographic prints of real wood. The former consists of genuine wood veneers laminated to a phenolic core which, with a melamine overlay, has the same practicality of standard plastic laminates. Do not use wood laminates with polyurethane or wax finishes for kitchen worktops.

Metallics

These are laminates using real metal foils over a laminate core to produce lightweight laminates which weigh far less compared with sheet metal. Some come with geometric patterned textures. NOTE that this type of laminate is suitable only for *light duty, vertical, interior surfaces.* However manufacturers are still developing new metallic laminates which they are confident will be suitable for work surfaces in the future.

Postforming

Most laminates can be postformed to bend over worktop front edges and over upstands at back of worktops. The usual recommended minimum internal radius is 10 mm, although some manufacturers can use a 3-mm radius which produces an almost square-edged look mimicking that of natural stone worktops.

Worktop manufacture and substrates

Plastic laminate worktops are always made in specialist workshops as it is difficult to achieve bubble-free bonding of the laminate to the substrate and to make perfectly mitred corner joints. Where worktops are made on site, advice should be sought from the manufacturer as to the most appropriate adhesive as these may vary from product to product.

The most suitable substrates for plastic laminates are moisture resistant chipboard, MDF and plywood as these are cellulose based with dimensional movement characteristics similar to those of decorative laminates.

Typical thickness is 28 or 38 mm. The underside and rear edge of the substrate should be faced with moisture resistant foil.

The most practical front edge profile is *bullnosed* or *double pencil round* where a postforming grade laminate is carried down the front face and back 15 mm underneath where it should meet the moisture resistant foil. This joint should be

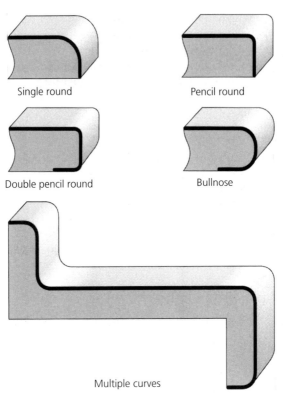

Single round

Pencil round

Double pencil round

Bullnose

Multiple curves

Front edge and Upstand profiles for plastic laminate worktops
by Spa Laminates

sealed with a silicone or resin seal. The distance of 15 mm is so that any drips from the front edge will fall on the face rather than the top edge of the cabinet doors below. See p. 160.

Front edges may also be lipped with hardwood or aluminium trim.
For a better, easy-to-clean, moisture-proof kitchen worktop, an integral upstand 75 to 100 mm high should be fixed to the back with the laminate taken up and round the top edge.
Holes for sinks, taps and hobs are generally best cut on site as the exact positions of these fittings can vary slightly from the drawings.

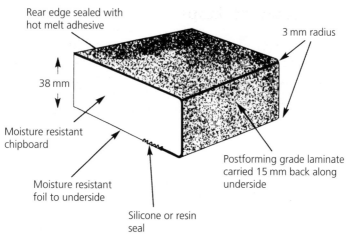

Rear edge sealed with
hot melt adhesive

3 mm radius

38 mm

Moisture resistant
chipboard

Moisture resistant
foil to underside

Silicone or resin
seal

Postforming grade laminate
carried 15 mm back along
underside

Typical postformed front edge detail to plastic laminate worktop

Other plastic laminate products

In addition to the standard decorative laminate sheets, there are also thicker sheets with a decorative face on both sides and a black or brown core. These are 3 to 20 mm thick and are primarily used for doors. Suitable also for worktops as it is very strong, high impact and moisture-resistant material.

They can also be postformed if required.

No substrates are needed over 6 mm thickness.

Recommended thickness for worktops is 10 mm.

Also available are solid colour melamine sheets 1.3 to 2.6 mm thick. These sheets can be glued together in layers, using epoxy adhesives, to make from 6 to 12 mm beautiful, hard-wearing and expensive work surfaces.

This product cannot be postformed but the surface can be routed, engraved or sand blasted.

Source: Formica Ltd

Hardwood worktops

Hardwood worktops are long lasting, hardwearing with great natural beauty. Timber seasons slowly and will darken with age. The main disadvantage to using hardwood for worktops is that it is important to avoid too much water sitting on the surface and it requires oiling from time to time to maintain water resistance.

Timber species

It is vitally important in today's concern about endangered species that all hardwoods are known to have come from a renewable source. The only safe guarantee that this is so is if the timber is certified by the *Forest Stewardship Council* (FSC). Consult the FSC for lists of accredited suppliers.

The following list describes the species that are considered suitable for domestic kitchen worktops.

Ash *Fraxinus Americana* from N. America
Light straw colour with occasional darker chocolate areas and strong textured grain. Suitable for worktops, but reacts more to moisture so must be well oiled in wet areas.

Bamboo *Phyllostachys pubescens*
Strips of thick straight stems, kiln dried, planed on all sides and glued together under pressure which can be worked like any hardwood. It is 27% harder than N. American red oak and 13% harder than maple. 3 m long × 30 mm thick available for worktops, it is kind to fabricators as the sawdust is heavy and falls to the ground.

Beech *Fagus sylvatica* from Germany and Romania
Straight, fine grained, pinkish-blond colour. Extremely hard and dense, but must be well oiled in wet areas.

Cherry *Prunus avium* from N. America and England
Excellent work surface material with some wavy grain which darkens from pale pink to reddish brown with the odd darker fleck. English varieties may have some green patina.

Iroko *Chlorophora excelsa* from W. Africa
Stable, solid timber which dramatically changes colour. Newly machined wood is very light with a distinctive buttery sheen which after several months changes to dark chestnut brown. Naturally oily and sometimes known as 'poor man's teak' it is none the less probably the best timber for kitchen worktops.

Mahogany *Swietenia macrophylla* from W. Africa
Reddish hardwood which matures to a rich dark colour in a few months. It has a fine texture which finishes to a very smooth surface. Grows to great heights so long lengths are obtainable.

Maple *Acer saccharum* from America and
            Acer pseudoplatanus (sycamore) from Europe
Traditionally used for work surfaces and end-grain butchers' blocks because of its dense, hard surface with a fine texture and even, creamy, pink-tinged colour. The European variety is less dense and heavy but has long been used for kitchen and dairy worktops.

Oak *Quercus alba* from England, France and N. America
Extremely strong and durable, mid-brown in colour with some grain figure with a few small flecks of red and white and occasionally small clean knots in long lengths. It has a high tannin content which can be drawn out and make dark stains if exposed to moisture, so care must be taken to keep it well oiled in wet areas.

Teak *Tectona grandis* from Burma
Now sadly an endangered species and so difficult and very expensive to obtain. It is also not popular with fabricators as it is grown in gritty soil which enters the timber and can ruin machine tools. It also contains a glutinous substance which makes it hard to work.

Walnut *Juglans nigra* from N. America
A quality timber with a blue-grey patina producing a dark finish when oiled. It is tough and finishes to a very high standard.

Construction

The best quality hardwood worktops are made up of *staves,* i.e. planks which vary in width from about 90 to 130 mm, depending upon species. They are held together with a finger joint and glued with water-resistant polyurethane adhesive.

maximum length: about 3.6 m
thickness: 30, 40 and 60 mm

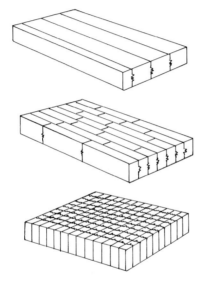

Top quality hardwood work-top made up of continuous staves 90–130 mm wide tongued and glued or finger jointed together

Standard hardwood worktop made up of 40 mm wide staves of various lengths

Endgrain worktop made up of staves glued together vertically in one direction and tongued and grooved in the other

Considerably cheaper hardwood worktops are made up of solid hardwood pieces 40 mm wide, comb-jointed and fixed with radio-frequency glue. As a result, this type of worktop will have a more varied colour and grain pattern than worktops made with continuous staves.

maximum length: 4.2 m
thickness: 27 and 40 mm

End grain worktops are made up of staves glued vertically with tongued and glued joints in one direction and butt joints in the other.

maximum size: 1 m^2
thickness: 40 to 150 mm

'L'-shaped worktops normally have straight butt joints so the grain of each leg will be at right angles to one another.
Diagonal joints are possible but more expensive as one leg will have to be longer and care must be taken to provide good support at the outside corner. Worktops are joined together using biscuits and bolts let into the underside.

Where timber worktops abut an Aga type range cooker, a *cross band* must be fixed to the end of the worktop to protect the end grain from the constant heat.

Front edges can be profiled as desired and holes cut for sinks, taps and hobs.

Draining grooves can be inserted next to sinks.
Stainless steel rods can be inserted slightly upstanding next to hobs as a rest area for hot pans.

If matching upstands at the back of the worktop are provided, then these must be fixed to the wall, NOT to the worktop to allow for differential movement.

Timber will always move in seasonal changes of humidity, so fixing hardwood worktops must allow for this. If possible arrange for the fixing to be done by the supplier.

The recommended finish is two or three coats of *Danish oil.* This oil is made up basically of Tung oil, some finishing oil and 2% urethane which provides the necessary water resistance. It is not a good idea to use polyurethane as a finish because if the surface is scored, moisture will penetrate the surface and lift the varnish. The oil also allows for the timber to move naturally.

Hardwood worktops should be re-oiled at regular intervals to keep them moisture resistant. When new, some areas may feel a little rough in the first few weeks of use as the grain lifts from the application of the oil. This can be made smooth with fine sand paper.

Source: Woodentops

Solid surface worktops

There are a range of man-made materials which resemble natural stones such as granite and limestone. They are made up of a composite of small chips of quartz, granite or aluminium trihydrate which is bound with pigments and resin or polyester resins.

The advantage of solid surface worktops over real stone is the possibility of having a large jointless surface of uniform colour and texture. They are said to be waterproof, hygienic, stable, durable, very hard, heat resistant to 180°C, stain resistant, colourfast indoors with a wide range of colours and patterns.

Very hot pans will scorch and bleach the surface. The marks can be removed once or twice with scouring powder. Undiluted bleach should not be left on the surface. Serious holes can be replaced with inserts to match by the fabricator.

Sheets suitable for kitchen worktops are generally 12–13 mm thick, bonded on to a substrate of MDF or plywood with the composite sheet covering the front edge which can be made to various profiles. Joints are solvent welded on site. Upstands at the back can be provided and some manufacturers make sink bowls which can be almost seamlessly welded to the worktop.

maximum length: 3.6 m
maximum width: 900 mm
thickness: 12 to 13 mm
weight: 24 kg/m²

Cost is about 85% that of natural stone worktops.

Solid surface worktops are easy to wipe clean.
Fine scratches can be smoothed with scouring powder or fine wet-and-dry sandpaper.

Stainless steel worktops

Stainless steel is the only material for serious long-term use for kitchen worktops. It is the preferred choice for commercial kitchens, primarily because the absence of allergens and toxic emissions makes it a most hygienic surface.

Stainless steel looks stylish and will remain good looking after many years of hard use.

It is easy to clean but will show limescale drips in hard water areas unless the water is softened. Very strong bleaches, silver-dipping liquid and strong acids may dull the surface.

Various round and rectangular, single and double sink bowls can be welded seamlessly to the worktops.

At least 35 mm must be kept between sink and worktop edge. 80 mm minimum must be allowed behind sinks for tapholes. Sound deadening panels are fitted to the underside of sink bowls to prevent drumming.

There are different front, back and side profiles to edge the worktop with a typical front edge being 20 or 30 mm high. At the back, upstands can rise up to 100 mm or be made with a small turn-up to receive wall tiles.

Worktops are mounted on 18 mm sealed blockboard substrate. L-shaped worktops are made in two pieces with a right-angled joint. The adjoining edges are turned down, bolted together from the underside with a silicone seal in the joint.

A textured finish is available for the whole surface of a work-top. This is said to facilitate drainage and mask scratches.

maximum length: 5 m
maximum width: 1.8 m
thickness: 1.25 mm standard, 1.0 mm textured finish
                 1.5 mm for acid resistance
weight: 21 kg/m^2
composition: 18/8 grade satin SS as standard

Source: GEC Anderson Ltd

Stainless steel worktop, sink and cabinets – by GEC Anderson Ltd

Concrete worktop
by Cast Advanced
Concretes

Hardwood worktop with SS under-
mounted sinks – by Second Nature

Stainless steel worktop
by Second Nature

Concrete worktops

Concrete for kitchen worktops is a relatively new product. It comes as a 40 mm thick slab made up of a 15 mm thick top surface with a 40 mm thick front downstand backed with a 25 mm MDF core which makes the slab less heavy and provides an easy surface for fixing from the underside.

The tops are factory made and finished with a two-part polymeric satin-finished sealant system which chemically bonds to the concrete and which the manufacturers claim makes it waterproof, alcohol resistant, UV stable, heat tolerant to 230°C with excellent wearing properties.

The colours available range from chalk-white through to limestone/sandstone colours to black.

maximum length: 3 m
maximum width: 1.2 m
thickness: 40 mm standard
                  30–100 mm also available
weight: 44 kg/m^2 for 40 mm thick slab

Concrete worktops will need good support to carry the weight.

Front edge profiles can have 3 mm *pencil-round* edges as standard or 45° *filed arrises* or be *bull-nosed.*

Holes cut for sinks and hobs must have at least 90 mm surrounding to maintain stability of the slab.

10 mm × 500 mm soft-edged draining grooves can be made for under-mounted sinks.

Source: Cast Advanced Concretes

Slate worktops

Slate is formed from the metamorphosis of sedimentary shale, clay and other minerals formed up to 590 million years ago.
It is exceptionally durable, unaffected by normal extremes of temperature, resistant to acid, alkalis and other chemicals, retains its colour, is waterproof and non-combustible.
Traditionally used for larder shelves and draining boards, it makes a handsome material for a kitchen worktop which is particularly suitable for pastry making due to its cool surface.

However, it is dark in colour ranging from dark blue-grey and heather-grey from Wales to green-grey from Cumbria – and will show up food residues and will not reflect light. Therefore slate worktops must be well-lit, both naturally and artificially.

Slate slabs for worktops are usually finished *fine rubbed* and polished *matt flat.* Exposed edges may be rubbed down to a *pencil round* or a *semi bull-nosed* profile.
At least 100 mm should be left round holes for sinks and hobs. If this is not possible, units can be made of smaller pieces, pre-drilled in joints for dowels and assembled on site.
Slate worktops are heavy and must be well supported

maximum length:	1.8 m – larger sizes may be available but are difficult to transport and install
maximum width:	900 mm
thickness:	25 mm as standard
weight:	71 kg/m^2 for a 25 mm thick slab

Slate needs no sealant and should not be oiled as it sits on the surface and gathers dust.

Wash with a neutral pH detergent, rinse and wipe dry. Scouring powders with abrasives may dull the surface. Minor scratches may be rubbed down with wet-and-dry sandpaper.

Source: Wincilate Ltd and Welsh Slate

Granite worktops

Granite is an igneous stone formed by cooling of molten rock far below the earth's crust over 5000 million years ago.

Its appearance is granular with crystals making a great variety of colours and textures. Colours range from pale grey through pink, red, yellow, brown, green to black.

For centuries it has been prized for its durability, hardness, density and impressive appearance when polished.

It is waterproof, stain resistant to all common liquids, very heat resistant, difficult to scratch and easy to keep clean.

If wine, oils and acidic products are left on the surface for a long time, they may stain or remove the polish and should be wiped off. Limescale removers should not be used.

Lighter colours tend to be cheaper than dark and also have the advantage of showing food and limescale deposits less.

Surfaces should be *highly polished* for kitchen use.

Avoid *honed matt* or *antiqued* finishes which may show stains and show up dirt.

Cut-outs for hobs, sinks and mixers should be undertaken by the fabricator. Front edges can have various profiles.

maximum length: 2.7 m
maximum width: 1.5 m
thickness: 30 mm without substrate
    20 mm with 22 mm MDF substrate
weight: 90 kg/m^2 for 30 mm thick slab
    65 kg/m^2 for 20 mm thick slab

Granite is heavy and will need strong support.

Joints have sawn edges with a slight arris to the top edge. They are glued together with a two-pack resin and hardener, coloured to match the granite and fill the groove made by the arrised edges. L-shaped worktops are joined at right angles.

Source: Granit-ops

Granite worktop with draining grooves for Belfast sink – by Second Nature

Solid surface worktop
with integral sinks with
SS bases – by Corian

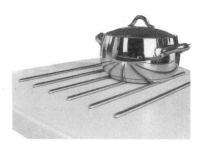

SS rods embedded into solid
surface worktop for pan rest
by Corian

Marble worktops

Marble is NOT recommended as a practical surface for kitchen worktops.
It is far less hard wearing than granite and will be stained badly by olive oil, lemon juice and spices.
It is, however, eminently suitable for use in bedrooms and bathrooms.

Limestone worktops

Limestone has recently become popular for wall and floor tiling and can be used for kitchen worktops, although it is not as suitable as other stones because it may be etched by acids such as lime juice. For this reason it is imperative to select a limestone of low porosity and maximum density. This type of limestone tends to come from Portugal, Spain, Italy and Israel.

The choice of finish is *fully polished* which cannot be sealed as sealants tend to sit on the surface. Alternatively, the surface can be *honed* which can take a polyurethane-type sealant which can be renewed professionally after some years of use.

Wash with a neutral detergent to keep it clean.
Scouring powders and cream cleaners should be avoided.

maximum length: 2.4 m
maximum width: 1.2 m
thickness: 30 mm recommended
20 mm will suffice with 6 mm MDF substrate fixed to top of cabinets
weight: 81 kg/m^2 for 30 mm
54 kg/m^2 for 20 mm

Upstands at the back edge should be fixed to the wall with a silicone joint between upstand and work surface.

Source: Kirkstone Quarries Ltd

16
Floor and wall finishes

Floor finishes for kitchens should be waterproof, hardwearing, non-slip when wet, easy to clean, acid- and alkali-proof and easy on the feet. Under traditional range cookers they should also be fireproof. They are better if they are pale in colour to reflect light, and slightly patterned to conceal grime.

Sheet materials have few joints so are easy to keep clean and are likely to be more waterproof – but tiles have the advantage of being easier to fit round awkward shapes and can be individually replaced if damaged.

In rooms which are not square, tiles laid on the diagonal disguise the fact that the walls are not parallel.

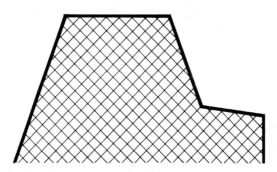

Tiles laid diagonally in a non-orthogonal location

It is preferable to use specialist flooring contractors who will advise on suitability of materials for the purpose, including details of any substrates, fixing, surface sealants or polishes. All flooring should be fixed and finished according to the manufacturer's instructions.

Timber floor finishes are NOT suitable for kitchens, even if well sealed, as water will eventually get underneath the seal and lift it off allowing the wood below to swell and discolour.

Described below are floor finishes which are suitable for domestic kitchen use. They divide basically into *soft* floor finishes which have the benefit of being quiet and kinder to feet, and *hard* floor finishes which are more durable but can be cold, noisy and hard on the feet. Hard finishes may also be more suitable for solid rather than suspended floors.

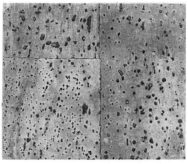

Cork tile – vinyl faced
300 × 300 × 3.2 mm – by Wicanders

Vinyl tile – 'Stones'
305 × 305 × 2 mm
by Harvey Maria

Linoleum tiles
500 × 500 × 2.5 mm
by Forbo-Nairn

Floor tiles – soft

Rubber stud tiles
503 × 503 × 3.2 mm
by Freudenberg

Soft floors

Vinyl flooring

Available in sheet or tile form with a vast choice of designs ranging from plain colours through random patterns to often very creditable imitations of natural materials. Generally vinyl floors are easy to keep clean with sweeping and washing. Some incorporate carborundum to make a lightly textured non-slip finish. These should be sealed to make them easier to clean.

typical sizes: 2 m rolls and 600 × 600 × 2 mm tiles.

Linoleum flooring

Linoleum is made from predominantly natural materials: linseed oil, rosin, wood flour and chalk backed with jute. It is environmentally friendly as it is largely emission free and non-allergenic. Its resilience makes it kind to feet, quiet and hard wearing.

typical sizes: 2 m rolls and 500 × 500 × 2.5 mm tiles.

Cork tiles – vinyl faced

This is one of the most practical and handsome floor finishes for a kitchen. It has the warmth, resilience and beauty of cork with the protection of a 0.5 mm clear vinyl sheet bonded on top as the wear layer. The random pattern of natural cork disguises dirt so effectively that the need for cleaning is only felt when one hears the sugar crunch underfoot, making it the perfect floor for the less than house-proud cook.

typical sizes: 300 × 300 × 3.2 mm tiles and
                 900 × 295 × 12 mm interlocking planks where
                 the cork is bonded to high density fibreboard with
                 an insulating layer of cork to the underside.

Sources: Armstrong, Forbo-Nairn, Freudenberg, Harvey Maria,
            Wicanders

Hard floors

Quarry tiles

Burnt clay tiles, typically red, heather, buff or black in colour, very dense and unglazed but less than 3% absorption. Also slip-resistant, scratch-hardy, easy to wash and keep clean particularly if finished with a proprietary clear acrylic polymer sealant which provides a satin gloss.

typical sizes: 150 × 150 × 12.5 mm square and octagonal
194 × 94 × 12.5 mm rectangular
194 × 194 × 12.5 and 18 mm
225 × 225 × 18 mm

The tiles are made with different surfaces: *plain*, *carborundum*, *shot-faced* (fine pimples), *studded*, giving varying degrees of non-slipperiness. There are special square tiles with *bull-nosed* edges to one or two sides and 100 mm high *coved* skirting tiles.

Slate tiles

Slate is durable, resistant to alkali, fade-proof, waterproof and non-combustible.

The tile finish should be *riven* to be non-slip.
It is hard and cold and, like all stone flooring, best with underfloor heating.

Being dark it will show up light-coloured spills but it is handsome and very hard wearing.
It helps to seal the tiles for easier cleaning.

typical sizes: 300 × 150 × 12 mm
300 × 300 × 12 mm
400 × 200 × 12 mm
500 × 500 × 12 mm
600 × 600 × 12 mm

Source: Welsh Slate

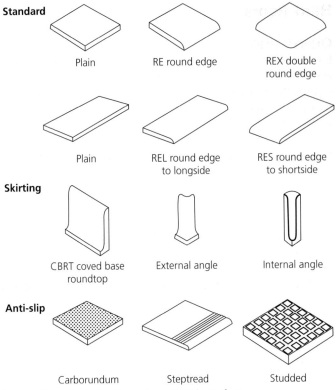

Standard

Plain   RE round edge   REX double round edge

Plain   REL round edge to longside   RES round edge to shortside

Skirting

CBRT coved base roundtop   External angle   Internal angle

Anti-slip

Carborundum   Steptread   Studded

Quarry tiles – typical patterns by – Dennis Ruabon

Ceramic tiles

Ceramic floor tiles can be glazed or unglazed.

If glazed they should have a lightly textured surface to make them more slip resistant and easy to clean.

Unglazed tiles should be *fully vitrified* which indicates they are practically non-porous, and should be sealed to make them easier to keep clean.

typical sizes: $150 \times 150 \times 8.5$ mm
$200 \times 200 \times 8.5$ mm
$200 \times 200 \times 12$ mm
$300 \times 300 \times 8.5$ mm
$400 \times 400 \times 10$ mm

Limestone tiles

Limestone is available in many light colours for floor tiles.
They are particularly attractive when used with a limestone worktop.
Choose the denser and least porous varieties for kitchen use. Tiles should be laid with white joints and finished with an appropriate sealant.

typical sizes: 305 × 305, 400 × 400, 600 × 600 mm
thickness: 10, 12, 15 and 20 mm

Source: Kirkstone Quarries

Terrazzo

A composite material developed in Italy where it is known as 'conglomerata' which has been used for floors since Roman times. It is made up of marble and other stone chippings set in a pigmented cement mix.

Terrazzo is only suitable for solid floors as the tiles are laid in mortar on a semi-dry concrete sub-base and ground and polished *in situ*.

It is good looking, hygienic with a variety of colours to order as each batch is purpose made.

As it is sealed at the time of laying, it needs no polishing and is easy to clean with water and a neutral detergent. The matrix may be slightly etched if acids and alkalis are not wiped off. After many years, it can be re-ground, grouted and polished.

Large areas can be laid wet with brass dividing strips, but for small kitchen areas, tiles are more appropriate.

Tile sizes: 300 × 300 × 28 mm
                  400 × 400 × 33 mm

Source: Quiligotti

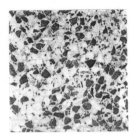

Terrazzo tiles
300 × 300 × 28 mm
by Quiligotti

Stainless Steel and aluminium tiles
300 × 300 bonded to various thicknesses of
tongued and grooved ply or MDF
by Metex Flooring

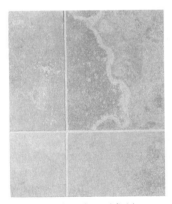

Limestone tiles – honed finish
400 × 400 × 12 mm
by Kirkstone Quarries

Slate floor tiles – riven finish
300 × 300 × 12 mm
by Welsh Slate

Floor tiles – hard

Stainless steel and aluminium flooring

Stainless steel and aluminium make a striking and durable floor finish for a kitchen.

The metals are available in various textures, some resembling chequer plate, which is necessary to make it non-slip.

Stainless steel is more hard wearing and costs about a third more than aluminium.

The finish can be *satin, brushed* or *bright.*
Aluminium must be *hard anodised.*
The finish can be *brushed, matt* or *shining.*

Both metals are available in sheet form, but tiles are easier to lay in small and awkward shaped areas. The metal is bonded on to MDF or marine ply with tongued and grooved joints which can be cut like a ceramic tile with a diamond tipped saw.

Tile size: 300 × 300 × 0.7 mm bonded on to 9, 12 or 15 mm tongued and grooved ply or MDF.

There are other stainless steel and aluminium tiles which are not bonded to a board but which can be stuck down to a sub-strate with a double-sided adhesive viscose sheet.

Tile size: 500 × 500 × 1.5 mm

The metals are not affected by acids, but bleach can dull the surface.

Normal cleaning is sweeping and washing.
Stubborn dirt can be removed with a product which is similar to a car-screen wash which removes dirt without leaving a greasy film.

Sources: Metex, THG International

Wall finishes

Kitchen walls have to cope with condensation and grease even when an efficient extractor fan is installed.

Walls behind hobs get particularly greasy.
Walls and window cills behind sinks are liable to get splashed.

Therefore these wall surfaces particularly between the work-top and wall cupboards and for at least 300 mm high above worktops elsewhere, should be protected with easy-to-clean materials such as:
ceramic tiles, mosaic, stainless steel sheet, plastic laminate-faced board, gloss-varnished timber matchboarding.

The latter should be protected with a sheet of laminated glass or stainless steel behind the hob as it may scorch.

For walls elsewhere, above tall cabinets for instance, gloss paint is easier to wash and longer lasting than matt emulsion.

17
Specification checklist

Summary of items which may need to be specified for a new kitchen

Demolition and preparation
(applicable where a kitchen is being installed in an existing room).
Making good to walls, floors and ceilings after demolition.
Alterations to existing doors, windows, making a hatch, fitting swing doors, cat flap.

Plumbing
Waste pipes, traps, hot and cold supply pipes, water softener, water filter, boiling and/or chilled water supply, stopcocks, connection to sinks, waste disposer, dishwasher and ice dispenser in refrigerator.
Gas pipes, stopcocks, connection to cooker/hob and ovens.
Sink unit and mixer.

Electrical
Wiring for socket outlets, connection units for appliances, cooker and water heater switches.
Wiring for lighting, telephone, entry phone, TV aerial, radio.

Ventilation
Air bricks/trickle ventilators for background ventilation.
Extract fan or cooker hood for hob.

Appliances
Provision of freestanding cooker/built-in oven(s), hob, microwave oven, cooker hood, dishwasher, waste disposer, refrigerator/fridge-freezer, freezer, wine cooler.

Cabinets   Base units, tall units, appliance housings, wall units, open shelves, cooker hood panel, end panels, plinths, lighting battens, pelmets, accessories for cabinet interiors, cabinet handles and hinges, wine rack, towel rail, etc.
Worktops.

Finishes   Floor finish, splashback for hob, wall and ceiling finishes.

Advisory organisations

Association of Manufacturers of Domestic Appliances (AMDEA)
Rapier House, 40 Lamb's Conduit St, London
WC1N 3NW
www.amdea.org.uk

tel: 020 7405 0666
fax: 020 7405 6609

Barbour Index Enquiry Service
New Lodge, Drift Road, Windsor SL4 4RQ
email: barbour-msc@cmpinformation
www.barbour-index.co.uk

tel: 01344 884121
fax: 01344 884113

British Electrotechnical Approvals Board (BEAB)
1 Station View, Guildford GU1 4JY
email: info@beab.co.uk www.beab.co.uk

tel: 01483 455466
fax: 01483 455477

British Stainless Steel Association (BSSA)
59 Clarkhouse Road, Sheffield S10 2LE
email: enquiry@bssa.org.uk www.bssa.org.uk

tel: 0114 267 1265
fax: 0114 267 1252

British Woodworking Federation
56 Leonard Street, London EC2A 4JX
email: bwf@bwf.org.uk www.bwf.org.uk

tel: 020 7608 5050
fax: 020 7608 5051

Building Centre
26 Store Street, London WC1E 7BT
email: information@buildingcentre.co.uk
www.buildingcentre.co.uk

tel: 020 7692 4000
fax: 020 7580 9641

Catering Equipment Suppliers Association (CESA)
235 Vauxhall Bridge Road, London SW1V 1EJ
email: enquiries@cesa.org.uk www.cesa.org.uk

tel: 020 7233 7724
fax: 020 7828 0667

Disabled Living Foundation
380 Harrow Road, London W9 2HU
email: dlfinfo@dlf.org.uk www.dlf.org.uk

tel: 020 7289 6111
fax: 020 7266 2922

Electrical Contractors Association
34 Palace Court, London W2 4HY
email: electricalcontractors@eca.co.uk
www.eca.co.uk

tel: 020 7313 4800
fax: 020 7221 7344

Federation of Master Builders
14 Great James Street, London WC1N 3DP
email: central@fmb.org.uk www.fmb.org.uk

tel: 020 7242 7583
fax: 020 7404 0296

Forest Stewardship Council UK
Unit D, Station Building, Llandidloes SY18 6EB
email: info@fsc-uk.org www.fsc-uk.org

tel: 01686 413916
fax: 01686 412176

Good Housekeeping Institute
72 Broadwick Street, London W1F 9EP   tel: 020 7439 5000
www.natmags.co.uk   fax: 020 7439 5591
Institute of Plumbing
64 Station Lane, Hornchurch RM12 6NB   tel: 01708 472791
email: info@plumbers.org.uk www.iphe.org.uk fax: 01708 448987
Institution of Electrical Engineers (IEE)
Savoy Place, London WC2R 0BL   tel: 020 7240 1871
email: postmaster@iee.org.uk www.iee.org.uk fax: 020 7240 7755
Kitchen Specialists Association
12 Top Barn Business Centre, Holt Heath WR6 6NH tel: 01905 621787
email: info@ksa.co.uk www.ksa.co.uk   fax: 01905 621887
Nat. Inspection Council for Electrical
Installation Contracting (NICEIC)
Vintage House, 37 Albert Embankment   tel: 020 7564 2323
London SE1 7UJ   fax: 020 7564 2370
Royal Institute of British Architects (RIBA)
66 Portland Place, London W1N 6AA   tel: 020 7580 5533
email: admin@inst.riba.org www.riba.org   fax: 020 7255 1541
Which?
P O Box 44, Hertford X, SG14 1SH   tel: 01992 822800
email: which@which.co.uk www.which.co.uk   fax: 020 7770 7485

Manufacturers and suppliers

AEG Domestic Appliances
55 High Street, Slough SL1 1DZ
www.aeg.co.uk
tel: 08705 158158
fax: 01753 538972

Aga-Rayburn
Station Rd, Ketley, Telford TF1 5AQ
email: info@aga-rayburn.co.uk
www.aga.rayburn.co.uk
tel: 01952 642000
fax: 01952 222048

AKW Medi-care
Severn House, Hylton Road, Worcester WR2 5JS
email: sales@akw-medicare.co.uk
www.akw.medicare.co.uk
tel: 01905 426500
fax: 01905 425413

Allmilmo UK
Unit 5, Rivermead, Pipers Way,
Thatcham RG19 4EP
email: allmilmo@aol.com
tel: 01635 868181
fax: 01635 869693

Alno UK Ltd
Unit 10, Hampton Farm Ind. Est,
Hanworth TW13 6AB
email: info-alno21@alno.co.uk
www.alno.co.uk
tel: 020 8898 4781
fax: 020 8898 0268

Amana
2 St Anne's Boulevard, Foxboro Rd,
Redhill RH1 1AX
www.amana.co.uk
tel: 01737 231000
fax: 01737 778822

Anaheim (UK) Ltd
Unit 1, 14 Camp Road, Farnborough GU14 6EW
email: contactus@anaheimuk.com
tel: 01252 408913
fax: 01252 408914

Anson Concise Ltd
1 Eagle Close, Arnold, Nottingham NG5 7FJ
email: info@ansonconcise.co.uk
www.ansonconcise.co.uk
tel: 0115 926 2102
fax: 0115 967 3398

Armitage Shanks
Armitage, Rugely WS15 4BT
email: info@thebluebook.co.uk
www.thebluebook.co.uk
tel: 01543 490253
fax: 01543 491677

Armstrong Floors
Hitching Ct, Abingdon Business Pk,
Abingdon OX14 1RB
www.armstrong-dlw.co.uk
tel: 01235 554848
fax: 01235 553583

Astracast plc
PO Box 20, Birstall WF17 9XD
email: marketing@astracast.co.uk
www.astracast.co.uk
tel: 01924 477466
fax: 01924 351297

Atag
173 Kenn Rd, Clevedon, Bristol BS21 6LH   tel: 01275 343000
email: sales@bradshaw.co.uk   fax: 01275 343454
www.bradshaw.co.uk
Avonite
Jenna House, N. Crawley Rd.   tel: 01908 210505
Newport Pagnell MK16 9QA   fax: 01908 210101
email: karenhudson@sylmar.co.uk
www.avonite.com
Baumatic Ltd
6 Bennet Road, Reading RG2 0QX   tel: 0118 933 6900
email: sales@baumatic.co.uk   fax: 0118 931 0035
www.baumatic.com
Belling
Glen Dimplex Cooking Ltd, Stoney La,   tel: 0151 426 6551
Prescot L35 2XW   fax: 0151 426 3261
www.bellingappliances.co.uk
BGL Rieber
Unit 6, Lancaster Industrial Estate,   tel: 01225 704470
Melksham SN12 6TT   fax: 01225 705927
email: sales @bglrieber.co.uk
Bisque Radiators
23 Queen Square, Bath BA1 2HX   tel: 01225 478500
email: mail@bisque.co.uk   fax: 01225 478586
www.bisque.co.uk
Blanco Ltd
Oxgate Lane, Cricklewood, London NW2 7JN   tel: 020 8450 9100
www.blanco.co.uk   fax: 020 8208 0095
Blum, Julius UK Ltd
Maidstone Rd, Kingston,   tel: 01908 285700
Milton Keynes MK10 0AW   fax: 01908 285701
email: info.uk@blum.com
www.blum.com
Bosch Domestic Appliances
Grand Union Ho. Old Wolverton Rd,   tel: 01908 328200
Wolverton MK12 5PT   fax: 01908 328560
www.boschappliances.co.uk
Brass & Traditional Sinks Ltd
Devauden Green, Chepstow NP16 6PL   tel: 01291 650738
email: sales@sinks.co.uk   fax: 01291 650827
www.sinks.co.uk
British Nova Works Ltd
Beaumont Road, Banbury OX16 1RB   tel: 01295 254030
email: sales@britishnova.co.uk   fax: 01295 254061
www.britishnova.co.uk
Bulthaup
1 North Terrace, Alexander Sq. London SW3 2BA   tel: 020 7317 6013
email: info@bulthaup.co.uk   fax: 020 7225 1770
www.bulthaup.co.uk

Calor Gas Ltd
Athena Drive, Tatchbrook Park, Warwick CV34 6RL   tel: 01926 330088
email: enquiry@calor.co.uk   fax: 01926 420609
www.calor.co.uk

Candy Domestic Appliances Ltd
New Chester Road, Bromborough, Wirral CH62 3PE   tel: 0151 334 2781
                                                  fax: 0151 334 9056

Care Design
Moorgate, Ormskirk L39 4RX   tel: 01695 579061
email: caredesign@clara.net   fax: 01695 570489
www.care-design.co.uk

Carron Phoenix Ltd
Carron Works, Stenhouse Road, Falkirk FK2 8DW   tel: 01324 638321
email: fgp-sales@carron.com   fax: 01324 620978
www.carron.com

Casdron Enterprises Ltd
Wood End, Prospect Road, Alresford SO94 9QF   tel: 01962 732126
email: sales@lithofin.co.uk   fax: 01962 735373
www.lithofin.com

Cast Advanced Concretes Ltd
Unit 4, Rempstsone Barns, Corfe Castle BH20 5JH   tel: 08702 418171
email: info@castadvancedconcretes.com   fax: 01929 481695
www.castadvancedconcretes.com

Commodore Kitchens
Acorn House, Gumley Road, Grays RM20 4XP   tel: 01375 382323
email: info@commodorekitchens.co.uk   fax: 01375 394955
www.commodorekitchens.co.uk

Commonfield Services Ltd
Unit 6, Redbourn Industrial Estate,   tel: 01923 260415
Redbourn AL3 7LG   fax: 01923 263574
email: sales@commonfield.co.uk
www.commonfield.co.uk

Concord marlin
Avis Way, Newhaven BN9 0ED   tel: 01273 515811
www.concord-lighting.com   fax: 01273 512688

Corian Solid Surfaces
McD Marketing Ltd, 10 Quarry Court,   tel: 01296 663555
Pitstone LU7 9GW   fax: 01296 663599
email: sales@corian.co.uk
www.corian.co.uk

Corner Fridge Company, The
Unit 6, Brunel Industrial Estate, Doncaster DN11 8SG   tel: 0845 061 6622
email: info@cornerfridge.com   fax: 01302 751233
www.cornerfridge.com

Countertops Ltd
Unit 5, Lymore Gardens, Bath BA2 1AQ   tel: 01225 424467
email: worktops@btconnect.com   fax: 01225 448107

Crabtree Kitchens
17 Station Road, London SW13 0LF   tel: 020 8392 6955
email: design@crabtreekitchens.co.uk   fax: 020 8392 6944
www.crabtreekitchens.co.uk

Creda
Morley Way, Peterborough PE2 9JJ   tel: 01733 456789
www.applied-energy.com   fax: 01733 310606
Crestwood Fittings Ltd
Crestwood Ho, St Martin's, Stamford PE9 2LG   tel: 01780 754407
email: enquiries@crestwood.co.uk   fax: 01780 752344
www.crestwood.co.uk
De Dietrich
Intec Four, Wade Rd, Basingstoke RG24 8NE   tel: 01256 843485
email: graham.ball@groupe.brandt.fr   fax: 01256 843024
www.brandt.com/uk
Dennis Ruabon Ltd
Hafod Tileries, Ruabon, Wrexham LL14 6ET   tel: 01978 843484
email: sales@dennisruabon.co.uk   fax: 01978 843276
www.dennisruabon.co.uk
Deralam Laminates Ltd
West Coast Park, Bradley Lane,   tel: 01257 478540
Standish WN6 0YR   fax: 01257 478550
email: sales@deralam.co.uk
Dimplex
Millbrook Ho, Grange Drive, Hedge End SO30 2DF   tel: 0870 077 7117
email: customer.services@glendimplex.com   fax: 0870 727 0109
www.dimplex.co.uk
Domus Tiles Ltd
1 Canterbury Ct. 6 Camberwell New Rd,   tel: 020 7091 1500
London SE5 0TG   fax: 020 7091 1501
email: service@domustiles.com
www.domustiles.com
Dornbracht
266 Brompton Road, London SW3 2AS   tel: 020 7589 9990
email: info@durante.co.uk   fax: 020 7589 9955
www.durante.co.uk
Ecoimpact Ltd
50a Kew Green, Richmond TW9 3BB   tel: 020 8940 7072
email: sales@ecoimpact.co.uk   fax: 020 8332 1218
www.ecoimpact.co.uk
EcoTile (UK) Ltd
The Old Print Works, 25 Tapster Street,   tel: 020 8449 1541
Barnet EN5 5TH   fax: 020 8440 2616
email: info@ecotile-uk.com
www.ecotile-uk.com
EcoWater Systems
Mill Rd, Stokenchurch HP14 3TP   tel: 01494 484000
email: info@ecowater.co.uk   fax: 01494 484396
www.ecowater.co.uk
Egger (UK) Ltd
Anick Grange, Hexham NE46 4JS   tel: 01434 602191
email: worktops@egger.com   fax: 01434 605103
www.egger.co.uk

Elite Trade Kitchens
90 Willesden Lane, Kilburn, London NW6 7TA   tel: 020 7328 1234
email: sales@elitekitchens.co.uk   fax: 020 7328 1243
www.elitekitchens.co.uk
Enerfoil Ltd
PO Box 2004 Aberfeldy PH15 2YF   tel: 01887 830638
email: sales@enerfoil.com   fax: 01887 830640
www.enerfoil.com
Excel Doors
Beaumont House, Allens Business Park,   tel: 01522 705111
Saxilby LN1 2LR   fax: 01522 705112
email: info@allensgroup.com
www.allensgroup.com
Fagor Electrodomesticos
Leroy House, 436 Essex Road, London N1 3QP   tel: 020 7354 0044
email: sales@fagorappliances.co.uk   fax: 020 7354 0789
www.fagorappliances.co.uk
Firstlight Products Ltd
22 Erica Rd, Stacey Bushes,   tel: 01908 310221
Milton Keynes MK12 6HS   fax: 01908 310229
email: flp@firstlight-products.co.uk
www.firstlight-products.co.uk
Fisher & Paykel
209 Purley Way, Croydon CR9 4RY   tel: 0845 600 1934
email: enquiries@fisherpaykel.co.uk
www.fisherpaykel.com
Forbo-Nairn Ltd
PO Box 1, Kirkcaldy KY1 2SB   tel: 01592 643777
email: headoffice@forbo-nairn.co.uk   fax: 01592 643999
www.forbo-nairn.co.uk
Fordham Appliances
PO Box 20, Birstall WF17 9XD   tel: 01924 351351
www.fordham-sinks.co.uk   fax: 01924 351333
Formica Ltd
Coast Road, North Shields NE29 8RE   tel: 0191 259 3000
email: samples@formica-europe.com   fax: 0191 258 2719
www.formica-europe.com
Franke UK Ltd
West Park, Styal Road, Manchester M22 5WB   tel: 0161 436 6280
email: info@franke.com   fax: 0161 436 2180
www.franke.co.uk
Freudenberg Building Systems UK Ltd
Unit 6, Wycliffe Ind. Pk. Leicester Rd,   tel: 01455 204483
Lutterworth LE17 4HG   fax: 01455 556529
email: norauk@freudenberg.com
www.nora.com
Frigidaire Consolidated Ltd
Express Way, Whitwood, Wakefield WF10 5QJ   tel: 01977 603111
email: sales@frigidaire.co.uk   fax: 01977 603159
www.frigidaire.co.uk

Gaggenau
Grand Union Ho. Old Wolverton Rd,   tel: 01908 328360
Milton Keynes MK12 5PT   fax: 01908 328360
www.gaggenau.com
GEC Anderson Ltd
Oakengrove, Shire Lane, Hastoe, Tring HP23 6LY   tel: 01442 826999
email: info@gecanderson.co.uk   fax: 01442 825999
www.gecanderson.co.uk
Genesis 1:3
Belvue House, Belvue Road, Northolt UB5 5QQ   tel: 020 8845 8444
email: sales@genesis1-3.co.uk   fax: 020 8845 7799
Granit-Ops
West Dean Road, West Tytherley, Salisbury SP5 1QG   tel: 01980 862253
email: stone@granit-ops.co.uk   fax: 01980 863073
www.granit-ops.co.uk
Häfele UK Ltd
Swift Valley Ind. Est. Rugby CV21 1RD   tel: 01788 542020
email: info@hafele.co.uk   fax: 01788 544440
www.hafele.co.uk
Hansgrohe
Unit D1, Sandown Pk Trading Est, Esher KT10 8BL   tel: 0870 770 1972
email: info@hansgrohe.co.uk   fax: 0870 770 1973
www.hansgrohe.co.uk
Hardall International Ltd
34 Clarke Road, Mount Farm,   tel: 01908 274441
Milton Keynes MK1 1LG   fax: 01908 367265
email: chutes@hardall.co.uk
www.hardall.co.uk
Harvey Maria
17 Riverside Business Park, Lyon Road,   tel: 020 8542 0088
London SW19 2RL   fax: 020 8542 0099
email: info@harveymaria.co.uk
www.norcool.com
Hettich UK
Unit 200, Metroplex Business Park, Salford M5 2UE   tel: 0161 872 9552
email: info@uk.hettich.com   fax: 0161 848 7605
www.hettich.com
H G Hagesan (UK) Ltd
Unit 11, Grange Way Business Park,   tel: 01206 795200
Colchester CO2 8HF   fax: 01206 795201
www.hginternational.com
Hotpoint
Celta Road, Peterborough PE2 9JB   tel: 01733 568989
email: info@hotpoint.com   fax: 01753 310606
www.hotpoint.co.uk
Ideal-Standard Ltd
The Bathroom Works, National Avenue,   tel: 01482 346461
Hull HU5 4HS   fax: 01482 445886
email: brochures@idea-lstandard.co.uk

In-Sink-Erator UK Ltd
6 The Courtyards, Croxley Business Park,   tel: 01923 296880
Watford WD18 8YH   fax: 01923 800628
email: insinkeratoruk@insinkerator.com
www.insinkerator.com
Isaac Lord
185 Desborough Rd, High Wycombe HP11 2QN   tel: 01494 462121
email: sales@isaaclord.co.uk   fax: 01494 510599
Jaymart Rubber & Plastics Ltd
Woodlands Trading Est. Eden Vale Rd,   tel: 01373 864926
Westbury BA13 3QS   fax: 01373 858454
email: matting@jaymart.net
www.jaymart.net
JCC Lighting Products
Beeding Close, Southern Cross Trading Est.   tel: 01243 829040
Bognor Regis PO22 9TS   fax: 01243 829051
email: sales@jcc-lighting.co.uk
www.jcc-lighting.co.uk
John Cullen Lighting
585 King's Road, London SW6 2EH   tel: 020 7371 5400
email: design@johncullen.co.uk   fax: 020 7371 7799
Jeld-Wen UK Ltd
1 Watch House Lane, Doncaster DN5 9LR   tel: 0870 1260000
email: marketing@jeld-wen.co.uk   fax: 01302 787383
www.jeld-wen.co.uk
Johnson, H & R Tiles Ltd
Harewood Street Tunstall, Stoke-on-Trent ST6 5JZ tel: 01782 575575
email: sales@johnson-tiles.com   fax: 01782 577377
www.johnsontiles.com
Junckers Ltd
Wheaton Road, Witham CM8 3UJ   tel: 01376 534700
email: sales@junckers.co.uk   fax: 01376 514401
www.junckers.com
Keep Able
Sterling Park, Pedmore Road,   tel: 01384 473719
Brierley Hill DY5 1TB   fax: 01384 473718
email: sales@keepable.co.uk
Keller Kitchens
340a Manchester Rd, W. Timperley,   tel: 0161 962 6939
Altrincham WA14 5NH   fax: 0161 962 6985
email: info.uk@kellereurope.com
www.kellereurope.com
Kirkstone Quarries Ltd
Skelwith Bridge, Ambleside LA22 9NN   tel: 01539 433296
email: info@kirkstone.com   fax: 01539 434006
www.kirkstone.com
Kitchenvision
The Coach Ho. 141 Hersham Rd,   tel: 01932 252458
Walton on Thames KT12 1RW   fax: 01932 252278
email: info@kitchenvision.co.uk
www.kitchenvision.co.uk

Küppersbusch UK
177 Milton Park, Milton, Abingdon OX14 4SE   tel: 01235 821288
email: info@kuppersbusch.co.uk   fax: 01235 831977
www.kueppersbusch.de

Lec Refrigeration plc
Shripney Road, Bognor Regis PO22 9NQ   tel: 01243 863161
email: frigepeople@lec.co.uk   fax: 01243 868052
www.lec.co.uk

Light Graphix Ltd
Vauxhall Place, Lowfield Street,   tel: 01322 222389
Dartford DA1 1HO   fax: 01322 271512
email: light@graphix.co.uk
www.lightgraphix.co.uk

M&G Olympic Products Ltd
109 Randall Street, Sheffield S2 4SJ   tel: 0114 275 6009
email: sales@mgolympic.co.uk   fax: 0114 273 9350
www.mgolympic.co.uk

Marley Floors Ltd
Dickley Lane, Lenham, Maidstone ME17 2QX   tel: 01622 854000
email: info@marley.com   fax: 01622 854500
www.marleyfloors.com

Max Appliances
Kingfisher House, Wheel Park, Westfield TN35 4SE   tel: 01424 751666
email: sales@max-appliances.co.uk   fax: 01424 751444
www.maxappliances.co.uk

Maytag UK
2 St Anne's Boulevard, Foxboro Rd,   tel: 01737 231000
Redhill RH1 1AX   fax: 01737 778822
www.maytag.co.uk

Mereway Ltd
Redfern Park Way, Birmingham B11 2BF   tel: 0121 706 7844
email: sales@mereway.co.uk   fax: 0121 706 6250
www.mereway.co.uk

Metex Flooring Systems Ltd
565 Duttons Way, Shadsworth Business Park,   tel: 01254 262610
Blackburn BB1 2PT   fax: 01254 262670
email: info@metalflooring.co.uk
www.metalflooring.co.uk

Miele Co Ltd
Fairacres, Marcham Road, Abingdon OX14 1TV   tel: 01235 554455
email: info@miele.co.uk   fax: 01235 554477
www.miele.co.uk

Mr Resistor
21 Lydden Road, London SW18 4LT   tel: 020 8874 2234
email: info@mr-resistor.co.uk   fax: 020 8871 2262
www.mr.resistor.co.uk

Myson Radiators Ltd
Eastern Avenue, Team Valley,   tel: 0191 491 7530
Gateshead NE11 0PG   fax: 0191 491 7568
email: sales@myson.co.uk
www.myson.co.uk

N & C Phlexicare Ltd
41 Freshwater Rd, Chedwell Heath RM8 1SP   tel: 020 8586 4600
email: info@nichollsandclarke.com   fax: 020 8586 4646
www.ncdirect.co.uk
Norcool
3 Albion Close, Newtown Business Park,   tel: 01202 733011
Poole BH12 3LL   fax: 01202 733499
email: sales@fdef.co.uk
www.norcool.com
Neff
Grand Union Ho. Old Wolverton Rd,   tel: 01908 328300
Milton Keynes MK12 5PT   fax: 01908 328560
www.neff.co.uk
New World
Glen Dimplex Cooking Ltd, Stoney Lane,   tel: 0151 426 6551
Prescot L35 2XW   fax: 0151 426 3261
www.newworldappliances.co.uk
Panasonic UK Ltd
Willoughby Road, Bracknell RG12 8FP   tel: 01344 862444
email: customer.care@panasonic.co.uk   fax: 01344 861656
www.panasonic.co.uk
Parapan
Thistle House, Gildersome Spur, Wakefield Rd,   tel: 0113 201 2240
Leeds LS27 7JZ   fax: 0113 253 0717
email: info@parapan.co.uk
www.parapan.co.uk
Pegler Hattersley
St Catherine's Avenue, Doncaster DN4 8DF   tel: 01302 560560
email: uksales@pegler.co.uk   fax: 01302 560109
www.peglerhattersley.com
Pilkington's Tiles Ltd
PO Box 4, Clifton Junction, Manchester M27 8LP   tel: 0161 727 1127
email: technical@pilkingtons.com   fax: 0161 727 1066
www.pilkingtons.com
Pland Stainless Ltd
Lower Wortley Ring Road, Leeds LS12 6AA   tel: 0113 263 4184
email: sales@plandstainless.co.uk   fax: 0113 231 0560
www.plandstainless.co.uk
Platt, Daniel Ltd
Brownhills Tileries, Tunstall, Stoke-on-Trent ST6 4NY   tel: 01782 577187
email: sales@danielplatt.co.uk   fax: 01782 577877
www.danielplatt.co.uk
Poggenpohl Group UK Ltd
681 Silbury Boulevard,   tel: 01908 247600
Central Milton Keynes MK9 1NR   fax: 01908 606958
email: kitchens@poggenpohl-group.co.uk
www.poggenpohl.de
Polished Metal Products Ltd
Devauden Green, Chepstow NP16 6PL   tel: 01291 650455
email: softoptions@sinks.co.uk   fax: 01291 650904
www.sinks.co.uk

Polyrey (UK) Ltd
49 Clarendon Road, Watford WD17 1HP   tel: 01923 202700
email: polyrey.uk.com   fax: 01923 202729
www.polyrey.com

Quiligotti Terazzo Ltd
PO Box 4, Clifton Junction, Manchester M27 8LP   tel: 0161 727 1000
email: quiligotti.sales@pilkingtons.com   fax: 0161 727 1006
www.quiligotti.co.uk

Redfyre Cookers
Osprey Rd, Sowton Industrial Estate, Exeter EX2 7JG   tel: 01392 444070
email: redfyre@gazco.com   fax: 01392 444804
www.redfyrecookers.co.uk

Ronseal Ltd
Chapeltown, Sheffield S35 2YP   tel: 0114 246 7171
email: trade@ronseal.co.uk   fax: 0114 245 5629
www.trade.ronseal.co.uk

Salamander (Engineering) Ltd
Reddicap Trading Est, Sutton Coldfield B75 7BU   tel: 0121 378 0952
email: sales@salamander-engineering.co.uk   fax: 0121 311 1521
www.salamander-engineering.co.uk

Schock UK Ltd
Unit 444, Walton Summit Centre,   tel: 01772 332710
Bamber Bridge PR5 8AT   fax: 01772 332717
email: sales@Schock.co.uk
www.schock.de

Second Nature worksurfaces
20 Station Road, Newton, Aycliffe DL5 6XJ   tel: 01325 505555
email: e.mail@PWS.co.uk   fax: 01325 505557
www.secondnaturecollection.co.uk

Siematic UK
Osprey Ho. Rookery Ct. Primett Rd.   tel: 01438 369327
Stevenage SG1 3EE   fax: 01438 368920
email: contract.sales@siematic.co.uk
www.siematic.com

Sissons, W & G Ltd
Carrwood Road, Sheepbridge, Chesterfield S41 9QB   tel: 01246 450255
email: wg@sissons.co.uk   fax: 01246 451276
www.sissons.co.uk

Smeg (UK) Ltd
3 Milton Park, Abingdon OX14 4RN   tel: 0870 990 9907
www.smeguk.com   fax: 0870 990 9337

Spa Laminates
59 Pepper Road, Leeds LS10 2TH   tel: 0113 271 8311
email: info@spalaminates.co.uk   fax: 0113 270 3968
www.spalaminates.co.uk

Space Savers (London) Ltd
222 Kentish Town Road, London NW5 2AD   tel: 020 7485 3266
email: enquiries@spacesavers.co.uk   fax: 020 7267 3256
www.spacesavers.co.uk

Staron (UK) Ltd
Haverton Ind. Est. Billingham,
Stockton-on-Tees TS16 0RW
email: enquiries@staron.co.uk
www.staron.co.uk
tel: 01642 565457
fax: 01642 562366

Steelplan Kitchens
Wealdstone Road, Kimpton Industrial Estate,
Sutton SM3 9RW
email: sales@steelplan.com
www.steelplan.com
tel: 020 8254 2018
fax: 020 8641 5026

Stoves
Glen Dimplex Cooking Ltd, Stoney La,
Prescot L35 2XW
www.stoves.co.uk
tel: 0151 426 6551
fax: 0151 426 3261

Strand, John (MK) Ltd
12 Herga Road, Wealdstone, Harrow HA3 5AS
email: enquiry@johnstrand-mk.co.uk
www.johnstrand-mk.co.uk
tel: 020 8930 6006
fax: 020 8930 6008

Sylmar Technology Ltd
Tickford House, Silver Street,
Newport Pagnell MK16 0EX
email: nick.butler@sylmar.co.uk
tel: 01908 210505
fax: 01908 210101

THG International Ltd
7 Shepherds Bush Rd, London W6 7NA
email: thgint@btinternet.com
tel: 020 7602 8057
fax: 020 7602 7516

Traditional Doors
Unit 12, Cradle Hill Industrial Estate,
Seaford BN25 3JE
tel: 01323 899944
fax: 01323 899955

Tweeny
Kingfisher House, Wheel Park, Westfield TN35 4SE
email: sales@tweeny.co.uk
tel: 01424 751888
fax: 01424 751444

U-Line Corporation
17 Mill Lane, Woodford Green, London IG8 0UN
email: sales@u-line.co.uk
www.u-line.co.uk
tel: 020 8506 6600
fax: 020 8505 8700

Vectaire Ltd
Lincoln Rd, Cressex Business Pk,
High Wycombe HP12 3RH
email: sales@vectaire.co.uk
www.vectaire.co.uk
tel: 01494 522333
fax: 01494 522337

Vent-Axia Ltd
Fleming Way, Crawley RH10 9YX
email: info@vent-axia.com
www.vent-axia.com
tel: 01293 526062
fax: 01293 551188

Villeroy & Boch (UK) Ltd
267 Merton Road, London SW18 5JS
www.villeroy-boch.com
tel: 020 8871 4028
fax: 020 8870 3720

Vola UK Ltd
Unit 12, Ampthill Business Pk, Station Rd,
Ampthill MK45 2QW
email: sales@vola.co.uk
www.vola.uk
tel: 01525 841155
fax: 01525 841177

Warmup plc
Unit 1, Rowley Industrial Park, Roslin Road,   tel: 0845 345 2288
London W3 8BH   fax: 0845 345 2299
email: technical@warmup.co.uk
www.warmup.co.uk

Welsh Slate
Unit 205, Business Design Centre, 52 Upper Street, tel: 020 7354 0306
London N1 0QH   fax: 020 7354 8485
email: enquiries@welshslate.com
www.welshslate.com

Whirlpool UK
209 Purley Way, Croydon CR9 4RY   tel: 020 8649 5000
email: whirlpool.uk@whirlpool.com   fax: 020 8649 5060
www.whirlpool.com

Wicanders
Star Road, Partridge Green, Horsham RH13 8RA   tel: 01403 710001
email: info.ar.uk@amorim.com   fax: 01403 710003
www.amorim.com

Wincilate Ltd
Aberllefenni Slate Quarries, Machynlleth SY20 9RU   tel: 01654 761602
email: slate@wincilate.co.uk   fax: 01654 761418
www.wincilate.co.uk

Woodentops
The Barn, Park Farm, Hundred Acre Lane,   tel: 01273 891891
Wivelfield Green RH17 7RU   fax: 01273 890044
email: sales@woodentops.co.uk
www.woodentops.co.uk

Woodfit
Kem Mill, Whittle le Woods, Chorley PR6 7EA   tel: 01257 266421
email: sales@woodfit.com   fax: 01257 264271
www.woodfit.com

World's End Tiles Ltd
202 Great Portland Street, London W1W 5QQ   tel: 0800 587 118
www.worldsendtiles.co.uk   fax: 020 7291 0741

Xpelair Ltd
Morley Way, Peterborough PE2 9JJ   tel: 01733 456789
www.applied-energy.com   fax: 01733 310606

Zanussi Ltd
55 High Street, Slough SL1 1DZ   tel: 01753 872500
www.zanussi.co.uk   fax: 01753 538972

Zehnder Ltd
B15 Armstrong Mall, Southwood Business Pk,   tel: 01252 515151
Farnborough GU14 0NR   fax: 01252 522528
email: sales@runtal-zehnder.co.uk
www.zehnder.co.uk

Zip Heaters
14 Bertie Ward Road, Rash's Green,   tel: 0870 608 8888
Dereham NR19 1TE   fax: 020 8870 3720
email: sales@zipheaters.co.uk
www.zipheaters.co.uk

Directory

Cabinets
Alno
Almilmo
Bulthaup
Crabtree
Crown Imperial
Elite
Keller
Nolte
Pogenpohl
Siematic

Cabinets, steel
GEC Anderson
M&G Olympic
Pland
Space Savers
Steelplan

Cabinets for the disabled
AKW Medicare
Care Design
Jeld-Wen
Keep Able
N&C Phlexicaire

Cabinet carcases
Jeld-Wen
Mereway
Woodfit

Cabinet doors
Commonfield
Crestwood
Excel
Mereway
Parapan
Traditional Doors
Woodfit

Cabinet fittings and accessories
Blum
Crestwood
Häfele
Isaac Lord
Woodfit

Cold rooms
Norcool

Cooking appliances
AEG
Aga-Rayburn
Atag
Baumatic
Belling
Bosch
Calor Gas
Candy

Creda
De Dietrich
Fagor
Fisher & Paykel
Gaggenau
Hotpoint
Küppersbusch
Maytag
Miele
Neff
New World
Redfyre
Smeg
Stoves
Whirlpool
Zanussi

Cooker hoods
AEG
Atag
Baumatic
Bosch
Creda
De Dietrich
Fagor
Gaggenau
Hotpoint
Maytag
Miele
Neff
New World
Smeg
Stoves
Vectaire
Whirlpool
Zanussi

Cooling appliances
AEG
Amana
Atag
Baumatic
Belling
Bosch
Corner Fridge
Creda
De Dietrich
Fagor
Fisher & Paykel
Frigidaire
Gaggenau
Hotpoint
Küppersbusch
Lec
Maytag
Miele
Neff
New World
Norcool
Smeg
Stoves
U-Line
Whirlpool
Zanussi

Dishwashers
AEG
Atag
Baumatic
Belling
Bosch
Candy
De Dietrich

Fagor
Fisher & Paykel
Gaggenau
Hotpoint
Küppersbusch
Maytag
Miele
Neff
New World
Whirlpool
Zanussi

Extractor fans
Vectaire
Vent-Axia
Xpelair

Floor finishes

Armstrong	vinyl
Dennis Ruabon	quarry tile
Domus	ceramic
Ecotile	vinyl
Forbo-Nairn	lino
Freudenberg	rubber stud
Harvey Maria	vinyl
Jaymart	rubber stud
Johnson	ceramic
Kirkstone	slate, limestone
Marley	vinyl
Metex	aluminium, SS
Platt, D	quarry tile
Pilkington	ceramic
Quiligotti	terrazzo
THG International	aluminium, SS

Welsh Slate	slate
Wicanders	vinyl-cork
Wincilate	slate
World's End	ceramic, stone

Freezers, see Cooling appliances

Heaters, electric

Dimplex	kickspace, etc.
Enerfoil	underfloor
Myson	kickspace
Warmup	underfloor
Zip	boiling and chilled water

Light fittings

Concord Marlin
Firstlight
Genesis
Hettich
JCC Lighting
John Cullen
Light Graphix
Mr Resistor

Microwave ovens

AEG
Atag
Baumatic
Bosch
Candy
Creda
De Dietrich
Fagor

Gaggenau
Hotpoint
Miele
Neff
Panasonic
Smeg
Whirlpool
Zanussi

Mini-kitchens (kitchenettes)

Anson
Space Savers
Steelplan
Strand

Plastic laminates

Deralam
Egger
Formica
Polyrey
Spa Laminates
Sylmar

Range cookers

AEG
Aga-Rayburn
Atag
Baumatic
Belling
Bosch
De Dietrich
Maytag
New World
Smeg
Stoves

Refrigerators, see Cooling appliances

Refuse compactors
Hardall
In-Sink-Erator

Sealants
British Nova
HG Hagesan
Ronseal

Sinks
Armitage
Astracast
BGL Rieber
Blanco
Brass & Traditional
Carron
Czech & Speake
Fordham
Franke
GEC Anderson
Ideal Standard
Pland
Schock
Sissons
Villeroy & Boch

Sink mixers
Armitage
Astracast
Blanco
Dornbracht
Hangrohe

Ideal-Standard
Pegler
Polished Metal
Vola
Zip

Towel radiators
Bisque
Myson
Zehnder

TV, CD and radio
Häfele
Kitchenvision

Wall tiles
Domus
Johnson
Pilkington

Waste bins
Häfele
Isaac Lord
Woodfit

Waste disposers
Anaheim
In-Sink-Erator
Max Appliances
Tweeny

Water softeners
Eco Water
Salamander

Worktops

Avonite	solid surface
Casdron	stone repairs
Cast Advanced	concrete
Corian	solid surface
Countertops	plastic laminate
Deralam	plastic laminate
Eco Impact	bamboo
Egger	plastic laminate
Formica	plastic laminate
GEC Anderson	stainless steel
Granit-Ops	granite
Junckers	hardwood
Kirkstone	slate, limestone
MG Olympic	stainless steel
Pland	stainless steel
Schock	solid surface
Second Nature	hardwood
Staron	solid surface
Steelplan	stainless steel
Sylmar	solid surface
Woodentops	hardwood

Wine coolers

Baumatic
Corner Fridge
Frigidaire
U-Line

Bibliography

Activities and Spaces: Dimensional Data for Housing Design
Noble, J. (ed)   AJ Supplement 1982
Aga – The Story of a Kitchen Classic
James, T.   Absolute Press 2002
Building Regulations 2000 Approved Documents
                        The Stationery Office (TSO) 2000–2004
The Building Regulations Explained and Illustrated
Powell-Smith, V. and Billington, M.J.   Blackwell Science
                                                      1995

The Cornell Kitchen
Beyer, G.H. (ed)   Cornell University 1955
Designing for Accessibility
                    Centre for Accessible Environments 1999
Good Housekeeping Kitchens
Austen, D. and Davies, C.   Ebury Press 1986
Good Housekeeping Microwave Encyclopaedia
Tee, S.   Ebury Press 1976
A Guide to the Security of Homes
Central Office of Information   HMSO 1986
The Home in Britain, The Shell Book of
Ayres, J.   Faber & Faber 1981
Home Security and Safety
Good Housekeeping Guide   Ebury Press 1995
The Kitchen Book
Conran, T.   Mitchell Beazley 1977
The Kitchen in History
Harrison, M.   Osprey 1972
Kitchens
Prizeman, J.   Macdonald & Co 1966

Kitchen Sense for disabled or elderly people
Ed. Sydney Foott   Disabled Living Foundation 1975
Kitchens Past and Present
Conran, T. (ed)   Hygena & Co 1976
Metric Handbook
Adler, D. (ed)   Architectural Press 1999
Planning: A Guide for Householders
Central Office of Information   DoE 1996
RIBA Product Selector
Young, S. (ed)   RIBA Enterprises 2004
Safety in the Home
DoE leaflet   HMSO 1976
Space in the Home
DoE metric edition   HMSO 1968
Spaces in the Home – Kitchens and Laundering Spaces
DoE   HMSO 1972

INDEX